EDINBURGH

Literary Lives & Landscapes

For Bernadette – with love

EDINBURGH

Literary Lives & Landscapes

D AVID C ARROLL

First published in 2004 by Sutton Publishing.
This paperback edition published in 2011 by

The History Press
The Mill, Brimscombe Port
Stroud, Gloucestershire, GL5 2QG
www.thehistorypress.co.uk

British Library Cataloguing in Publication Data.
A catalogue record for this book is available from the British Library.

ISBN 978 0 7524 6214 1

Typesetting and origination by The History Press
Printed and bound in Great Britain by
Marston Book Services Limited, Didcot

CONTENTS

LIST OF ILLUSTRATIONS

Black and white plates between pages 52 and 53

Photographs 1, 3, 5, 6, 11, 13, 14, 18, 21, by courtesy of Edinburgh City Libraries; no. 17, by courtesy of Corporate Services, Napier University; no. 25, by courtesy of the Director, Edinburgh International Book Festival; nos 2, 7, 8 and 19 were drawn from private collections. All other photographs were taken by the author.

PREFACE

Outside London, Edinburgh can surely boast the richest literary heritage of any major city in Britain. Standing on the sometimes windswept south bank of the Firth of Forth, and presided over by an ancient castle and the extinct volcano of Arthur's Seat, the spacious Georgian streets and squares of Edinburgh's New Town, coupled with the tenements and narrow wynds of its historic Old Town, have echoed down the centuries with the footsteps of world-famous native writers such as Sir Walter Scott, Robert Louis Stevenson and Sir Arthur Conan Doyle. There have been many illustrious literary visitors too, including Samuel Johnson, Robert Burns and Charles Dickens. Meanwhile, other famous authors – Thomas Carlyle and J.M. Barrie among them – were drawn to the city in their youth to study at Edinburgh's venerable university.

My aim in this book is to explore the lives of many of those writers who, over the years, have to a greater or lesser degree forged a link with Edinburgh and to demonstrate, where appropriate, how that connection influenced – or was reflected in – their work. The result, I hope the reader will agree, has been to throw some light on the literary landscape of what many people still regard as the most elegant of cities.

Before we proceed I must point out that anyone delving into Edinburgh's literary heritage owes a great debt to the work of two authors in particular: Trevor Royle, whose *Precipitous City* appeared in 1980, and Andrew Lownie, whose *Literary Companion to Edinburgh* was re-issued in 2000.

I have received help from many quarters during the preparation of this book. I am particularly grateful to Joan Lingard and Jenny Brown for talking to me at some length about the history of the Edinburgh International Book Festival; to Sarah Bryce at Sutton Publishing for her guidance; to my wife Bernadette Walsh for the time she spent researching and typing on my behalf (and for suggesting many of the chapter titles); to Andrew Bethune of the City Libraries' Edinburgh Room and Alan Shedlock of Napier University for locating archive photographs; to Ian Ball and Richard Stenlake for other photographic assistance; and to the staff of Lochthorn Library, Dumfries, for their unfailing help. Finally, this book was completed despite the distractions of Sam and Toby who, each in their own special way, hindered my progress at every turn.

David Carroll
Shieldhill, 2004

ACKNOWLEDGEMENTS

I am grateful to the following for permission to quote extracts from copyright material:

'What Images Return' in *Memoirs of a Modern Scotland* (ed. Karl Miller, Faber & Faber, 1970), *Curriculum Vitae* (Constable, 1992) and *The Prime of Miss Jean Brodie* (Penguin, 1961), the respective publishers, Muriel Spark and David Higham Associates; *The Greenwood Hat* (Peter Davies, 1937), *An Edinburgh Eleven* (1889), *Margaret Ogilvy* (1896), *Letters of J.M. Barrie* (ed. Viola Meynell, Peter Davies, 1942), speeches made by J.M. Barrie in 1896 and 1926, an article written by J.M. Barrie for the *Nottingham Journal* in 1883, a letter from J.M. Barrie to Sylvia Llewelyn Davies in 1909 and *Portrait of Barrie* (James Barrie, 1954) by Lady Cynthia Asquith, Samuel French Ltd on behalf of the Estate of J.M. Barrie; *Rebecca West. A Life* (1987), Victoria Glendinning and Weidenfeld & Nicolson; *Lives of the Poets* (Weidenfeld & Nicolson, 1998), Michael Schmidt © Michael Schmidt 1998; *Compton Mackenzie: A Life*, Andro Linklater (Chatto & Windus, 1987), used by permission of the Random House Group Ltd; *The Journal of Sir Walter Scott* (ed. W.E.K. Anderson, 1972), reprinted by permission of the editor and Oxford University Press; James Boswell's *Edinburgh Journals 1767–86* (ed. Hugh M. Milne, 2001 edn), Mercat Press Ltd; *John Buchan by His Wife and Friends* (ed.

ACKNOWLEDGEMENTS

Lady Tweedsmuir, Hodder & Stoughton, 1947), *Memory Hold-the-Door*, John Buchan (Hodder & Stoughton, 1940), A.P. Watt Ltd on behalf of the Lord Tweedsmuir and Jean, Lady Tweedsmuir; 'Man and Roy' in *Scotland on Sunday* (August 2002), Roy Hattersley; *The Kiss* (2002), Joan Lingard and Allison & Busby, London; *The Judge* by Rebecca West (Copyright © Rebecca West, 1922), by permission of PFD on behalf of the Estate of Rebecca West; *Edinburgh* by Eric Linklater (Copyright © Eric Linklater 1960), by permission of PFD on behalf of the Estate of Eric Linklater; lines from 'Edinburgh Courtyard in July' and 'Milne's Bar' from *Collected Poems* by Norman MacCaig (Chatto & Windus, 1985), reproduced by permission of Polygon, an imprint of Birlinn Ltd; *Wilfred Owen*, Jon Stallworthy (OUP, 1977 edn) and *Wilfred Owen: Collected Letters* (ed. Harold Owen and John Bell, OUP, 1967), reprinted by permission of Oxford University Press; J.A. Froude's *Life of Carlyle* (ed. John Clubbe, 1979), John Murray (Publishers) Ltd; *My Life and Times: Octave Ten*, Compton Mackenzie (Chatto & Windus, 1971), the Society of Authors as the Literary Representative of the Estate of Compton Mackenzie; *Siegfried's Journey* (Faber & Faber, 1945), *Sherston's Progress* (Faber & Faber, 1936) and an extract from Siegfried Sassoon's 1917 Declaration, Copyright Siegfried Sassoon, by kind permission of George Sassoon; Claire Harman's essay on Robert Louis Stevenson in *Writers and their Houses* (ed. Kate Marsh, Hamish Hamilton, 1993), The Penguin Group (UK); *Charles Dickens*, Una Pope-Hennessy (Chatto & Windus, 1945), used by permission of the Random House Group Ltd; *The Carlyles at Home*, Thea Holme (OUP, 1979 edn), reprinted by permission of Oxford University Press; the editor of *The Bookseller* for an extract from Tony Gould Davies's letter in the issue dated 15 January 1983. Attempts to trace the copyright holder of *A Flame in Sunlight*, Edward Sackville-West (Cassell & Co. 1936) and of *The Story of J.M.B.*, Denis MacKail (Peter Davies, 1941) have proved unsuccessful. Any omissions from the above list are entirely unintentional, and I would be pleased to rectify them (upon notification) in any subsequent edition of this work.

one

BOSWELL AND JOHNSON
A Man led by a Bear

On 16 May 1763, during one of his frequent and protracted visits to London, the future biographer James
Boswell was visiting the Russell Street bookshop owned
by his actor friend Thomas Davies in the Covent Garden district
of the capital, when in through the doorway stepped the
illustrious Samuel Johnson, thus setting in train one of the most
celebrated of literary friendships in the entire history of English
letters. Nearly two and a half centuries later their names are
still inextricably linked – Boswell's peerless biography, *The Life
of Samuel Johnson*, has been regarded as a literary masterpiece
ever since its first appearance in 1791 – but, on the face of
it, this was one of the unlikeliest of liaisons: the 22-year-old
offspring of a landed Ayrshire family falling under the spell of
the Staffordshire bookseller's son who was more than thirty
years his senior.

At the time of their first meeting, Lichfield-born Johnson
was already a considerable literary celebrity, following the
publication of his ground-breaking *Dictionary of the English
Language* in 1755, a work of enormous scholarship and
erudition that had taken him nearly ten years to complete. He

was also a poet, critic, biographer, and a dauntingly prolific essayist.

Boswell, on the other hand, had still to make his way in the world. Born on 29 October 1740 in Edinburgh's Parliament Close (later renamed Parliament Square), which lies at the rear of St Giles's Cathedral, he was educated at James Mundell's school in the nearby West Bow but with the added advantage of having private tutors at home. Boyhood illness had sent him south to Dumfriesshire and the famous eighteenth-century spa resort of Moffat which, in those days, was firmly established as 'the Cheltenham of Scotland'. Here, for better or worse, the young Boswell duly 'took the waters' (which, according to one local guide book, tasted like 'the scourings of a foul gun').

The Edinburgh of Boswell's day was much smaller, of course, than the present city. Although the area now known as the New Town, to the north of Princes Street, had begun to be developed during Boswell's lifetime, he was born and grew up in the Old Town. This was a district characterised by tenement buildings and narrow streets and wynds that, in the early eighteenth century, even the mildest of critics would have been forced to describe on the whole as crowded, smoky and above all noisome. 'The city suffers infinite disadvantages', noted Daniel Defoe in his *Tour through the Whole Island of Great Britain* (1724–6), after visiting Edinburgh in the early 1700s, 'and lies under such scandalous inconveniences as are, by its enemies, made a subject of scorn and reproach; as if people were not as willing to live sweet and clean as other natives, but delighted in stench and nastiness . . . Though many cities have more people in them, yet, I believe, this may be said with truth, that in no city in the world so many people live in so little room as at Edinburgh.'[1]

Captain Edward Topham, an army officer serving in the Guards, visited Edinburgh during 1774 and, in a series of letters written to his family at home in England, describes what he saw of the New Town taking shape. 'The greatest part of the New Town is built after the manner of the English,' he observed, 'and the houses are what they call here "houses to themselves". Though this mode of living, one would imagine, is much preferable to the former, yet such is the force of prejudice, that there are many people who prefer a little dark confined tenement on a sixth storey to the convenience of a whole house . . . In no town that I ever saw can such a contrast be found betwixt the ancient and modern architecture . . .'[2]

Although the age of Edinburgh's great literary celebrity on the international stage – which perhaps reached its zenith with the reign of Sir Walter Scott – was a thing of the future when Boswell was growing up in the city, the poet Allan Ramsay was still alive (living in his octagonal retirement home nicknamed 'Goose Pie House' on Castlehill, where Ramsay Garden can be found today) and, from the group of Court poets who had flourished in Edinburgh during an earlier period, Boswell would have undoubtedly been familiar with the work of William Dunbar.

Little is known about Dunbar's life, except that he was probably born in East Lothian in about 1460 and educated at St Andrews University. He certainly became a well-travelled man for his time, visiting the Courts of England and France and, according to his late nineteenth-century biographer, Oliphant Smeaton, '. . . travelling all over Europe from the banks of the Tiber . . . to those of "cauld Norway over the faem" . . .' But, as Smeaton continues, 'Like Samuel Johnson towards Fleet Street, William Dunbar considered the High Street and the Canongate of Edinburgh the fairest spots on earth . . . and to [him] the scenes which he daily witnessed in the busy, dirty, crowded malodorous streets of the capital . . . had a charm infinitely more fascinating than the matin-song of birds, heard in some leafy grove, [or] than the slumber of the summer sunshine on the green Pentland slopes, over which the cloud-shadows flitted like the voiceless spirits of the past . . .'[3]

Dunbar's most famous work was possibly 'The Thrissil and the Rois' (1503), an allegorical poem relating to the marriage of Margaret Tudor and James IV, but his hard-hitting 'Address to the Merchants of Edinburgh' evokes the city he loved so well:

> Quhy will ye merchantis of renoun,
> Lat Edinburgh, your nobil toun,
> For laik of reformatioun
> The commone proffeitt tyine and fame?
> Think ye not schame,
> That onie uther regioun
> Sall with dishonour hurt your name . . .

By the time he met Johnson, Boswell had been a student at both Edinburgh and Glasgow Universities, and was then studying the law under the supervision of his father, the Scottish judge Lord Auchinleck (the name derived from the family estate), although his heart leaned more towards literature and the theatre. He had already started to write and publish ephemeral verses, and had also befriended a number of actors and writers. These included Thomas Davies, the Russell Street bookseller, and, by coincidence, one of Johnson's former pupils from his early days as a schoolmaster, the actor David Garrick. As Davies and Johnson were friends, it is not entirely surprising that the great man should put in an appearance at the bookshop while Boswell was present.

At first, Boswell was made slightly apprehensive by the knowledge that Johnson harboured a prejudice against Scotland and its people, but in the event this proved no barrier to their forming a friendship. 'I was highly pleased with the extraordinary vigour of [Johnson's] conversation,' Boswell confided to his journal after their initial meeting, 'and had ventured to make an observation now and again which he received very civilly; so that I was satisfied that though there was a roughness in his manner, there was no ill-nature in his disposition. Davies followed me to the door and when I complained to him a little of the hard blows which the great man had given me [on account of being Scottish] he kindly took upon him to console me by saying, "Don't be uneasy. I can see he likes you very well."' Boswell also described Johnson's 'most dreadful appearance . . . He is a very big man, is troubled with sore eyes, the palsy and the King's Evil [scrofula]. He is very slovenly in his dress and speaks with a most uncouth voice. Yet his great knowledge and strength of expression command vast respect and render him very excellent company.'[4]

A few months later Boswell left London, bound for Holland. From there he travelled in Germany and subsequently visited Italy and Corsica before returning to Edinburgh in 1766 and passing his examination in Scots law. For almost the next twenty years he practised diligently in the city as an advocate at the Scottish Bar. In the meantime, however, he retained his keen interest in all things theatrical and literary and, during his almost annual visits to London, his friendship with the irascible Johnson strengthened. From almost the first time they met, Boswell had been urging the famous lexicographer to master his self-confessed antipathy to Scotland and come and view the country for himself. Ten years were to elapse, however, before Johnson could be finally prised from the taverns and coffee-houses that were among his favourite London haunts to make the long journey north in the summer of 1773; at the age of sixty-four it was the first time he had ventured so far from home.

By now, Boswell was married to his cousin Margaret Montgomerie and living in a well-appointed flat in James's Court (the birthplace in the 1960s of the Traverse Theatre) in Edinburgh's Lawnmarket. Their daughter, Veronica, was just five months old, but neither marriage nor the novelty of fatherhood had done much to change Boswell's habitual lifestyle. His new status as a family man signally failed to dampen his casual interest in other women, nor did it curb his frequently recurring bouts of heavy drinking, as his diary from that period amply testifies. 'A great deal of wine was drank [sic] today,' runs one typical entry. 'I swallowed about a bottle of port, which inflamed me much, the weather being hot . . . [Later] I devoured moor-fowl, and poured more port down my throat. I was sadly intoxicated.' The following day's entry is all too predictable. 'I was very sick and had a severe headache, and lay between ten and eleven, when I grew better.' On another occasion, after drinking heavily, 'I ranged the street and followed whores . . .', although contrition had set in by the next morning. 'My riot had distressed me terribly . . . I was so ill today that I could not rise.'[5]

On 3 August 1773 Johnson informed Boswell: 'I shall set out from London on Friday the sixth of this month, and purpose not to loiter much by the way. Which day I shall be at Edinburgh I cannot exactly tell. I suppose I must drive to an inn, and send a porter to find you . . .'[6] Johnson was as good as his word and, after travelling by way of Berwick-upon-Tweed, he appeared in the late evening of Saturday 14 August at Boyd's Inn off the Canongate. Boswell duly describes his friend's long-awaited arrival in *The Journal of a Tour to the Hebrides* (1785), his account of their subsequent three months' Scottish journey together: 'I went to him directly. He embraced me cordially; and I exulted in the thought that I now had him actually in Caledonia . . . He was to do me the honour to lodge under my roof . . . and [we] walked arm-in-arm up the High Street to my house in James's Court. It was a dusky night; I could not prevent his being assailed by the evening effluvia of Edinburgh. I heard a late baronet . . . observe that "walking the streets of Edinburgh at night was pretty perilous, and a good deal odoriferous." The peril is much abated, by the care which the magistrates have taken to enforce the city laws against throwing foul water from the windows; but from the structure of the houses in the old town, which consist of many stories [sic], in each of which a different family lives, and there being no covered sewers, the odour still continues. A zealous Scotsman would have wished . . . Johnson to be without one of his five senses upon this occasion. As we marched slowly along he grumbled in my ear, "I smell you in the dark!" But he acknowledged that the breadth of the street, and the loftiness of the buildings on each side, made a noble appearance.'[7]

Edward Topham, who stayed in Edinburgh the following year, graphically described how, away from public view in the narrow wynds leading off the High Street, many citizens, despite the threat of fines or harsher punishments, persisted in defying the magistrates' ruling. 'Many an elegant suit of clothes has been spoiled,' he lamented, 'and many a well-dressed macaroni sent home for the evening and, to conclude . . . in Dr. Johnson's own simple words "many a full-flowing periwig moistened into flaccidity."'[8]

Johnson was a self-confessed 'hardened and shameless tea-drinker, who has, for many years, diluted his meals with only the infusion of this fascinating plant; whose kettle has scarcely time to cool; who, with tea amuses the evening, with tea solaces the midnights, and with tea welcomes the morning'.[9] Bearing this in mind, Boswell had made certain that his wife would be ready with the teapot to welcome their distinguished guest on his arrival in a fashion that he would appreciate. '[Johnson] showed much complacency upon finding that the mistress of the house was so attentive to his singular habit,' recorded Boswell, 'and as no man could be more polite when he chose to be so, his address to her was most courteous and engaging . . .'[10]

The Boswells' flat was a positive hive of activity during the four days that Johnson made it his headquarters before setting out with his friend on their long journey to the Hebrides. Johnson's national celebrity meant that he was fêted wherever he went in the country and Edinburgh proved no exception. Johnson, much to Mrs Boswell's dismay, it seems, was 'at home' to a constant stream of visitors, many of whom were drawn from Edinburgh's literati, and who wished to pay their respects in person to the man who was widely known as 'Dictionary Johnson'.

Mrs Boswell, it has been suggested (not least by Johnson himself), did not greatly relish the company of her husband's highly respected friend, whose brief – but, as far as she was concerned, all too lengthy – presence could hardly have done other than to dominate the James's Court flat. When at home in London, Johnson habitually lived in a state of domestic chaos; he was a large man whose ungainly body with its host of tics and involuntary movements was best given free rein in the great outdoors, rather than in the confines of someone else's home. Not surprisingly, he jarred Mrs Boswell's nerves and threw more than one spanner in the works of her domestic arrangements. His tendency to upset candles and spill wax on the carpets was, according to Boswell, the habit that annoyed her most of all.

It must have been the source of some relief to the beleaguered Mrs Boswell, therefore, when her husband occasionally winkled the portly Johnson out of their home to view some of Edinburgh's finer sights, including the Parliament House, St Giles's and, inevitably, the castle and the Palace of Holyroodhouse, the last two being ports of call that no present-day tourist worth their salt would ever leave Edinburgh without visiting. Almost wherever Johnson went a knot of interested spectators gathered around him and followed where he led. Calling upon his deepest reserves of stamina, he also made his way to the top of Edinburgh's tallest building, which was thirteen storeys high.

On the morning of Wednesday 18 August, Boswell and Johnson left Edinburgh at the start of their epic tour; one that would take them – among other places – as far north as the Moray Firth and westwards to the Inner Hebridean islands of Skye, Raasay and Coll. Their journey, frequently made over the roughest of terrain on foot and horseback, carried them to some of Britain's wildest and most remote spots, before leading them back to Edinburgh three months later, on 9 November, when once again Johnson was billeted at his friend's flat in James's Court. This meant a further interlude of general disruption to her household for Mrs Boswell, and another procession of visitors dropping in and out all day long to see her famous guest, but she weathered the storm stoically if not altogether silently. In a widely quoted remark, she waspishly declared that she had 'often seen a bear led by a man but I never before saw a man led by a bear', an observation that leaves no doubt about her feelings on the subject of her husband's friendship with Johnson.

The social whirl, of which Johnson formed the epicentre, continued unabated. 'On the mornings when he breakfasted at my house,' recorded Boswell, 'he had, from ten o'clock till one or two, a constant levee of various persons, of very different characters and descriptions. I could not attend him, being obliged to be in the Court of Session; but my wife was so good as to devote the greater part of the morning to the endless task of pouring out tea for my friend and his visitors. Such was the disposition of his time at Edinburgh.' Johnson complained at one stage of having been 'harassed by invitations' before acknowledging 'how much worse it would have been if we had been neglected'.[11]

Johnson, perhaps keen to return to London before the worst weather of the winter set in, left Edinburgh in late November, never to return. Surprisingly, in his own account of his Scottish jaunt, *A Journey to the Western Islands of Scotland* (1775), he dismissed Edinburgh out of hand in the second paragraph as 'a city too well known to admit description'.[12]

Boswell owes his literary celebrity to Dr Samuel Johnson. Captivated from the start of their acquaintance by his friend's personality and unparalleled powers of conversation, the Edinburgh advocate had been gathering information and material for a possible biography ever since the occasion of their first meeting in 1763.

After Johnson's departure from James's Court, the two friends continued to meet in London from time to time just as before, while Boswell carried on practising the law in Edinburgh.

However, following Johnson's death in December 1784, Boswell's work on his friend's biography accelerated, and he devoted an increasing amount of his energy to assembling for the press the vast wealth of material that he had gathered over the years. Now spending much of his time in London, Boswell moved to the capital permanently in 1786, eventually settling at a house in what was then the fashionable quarter of Great Portland Street. Boswell's *Life of Samuel Johnson* was finally published in 1791, just four years before its author's death. Boswell's infinitely painstaking labours over the book – 'Let me only observe, as a specimen of my trouble,' he wrote in the Introduction to its first edition, 'that I have sometimes been obliged to run half over London in order to fix a date correctly'[13] – were duly rewarded. For over two hundred years this celebrated biography has remained the benchmark of its kind. Boswell was the author of several other books, including his *Account of Corsica* (1768) and *The Journal of a Tour to the Hebrides* (1785), which gave readers a foretaste of the biography that was to come. He was a noted diarist and essayist (between 1777 and 1783 he contributed many articles to *The London Magazine* using the pseudonym 'The Hypochondriak'), but his *Life of Samuel Johnson* remains his single greatest achievement.

'[Boswell] had all the weaknesses that afflict mankind,' concluded the novelist Eric Linklater. 'He was vain and foolish, drunken and lecherous, an ardent snob – and despite his weaknesses, or because of them, he wrote with genius and created a masterpiece. Not many men have been quite as silly as Boswell; and very few have made such good use of their lives, or written so well.'[14]

two

ROBERT BURNS
A Meteor Appearance

Robert Burns was twenty-seven when he arrived in Edinburgh during the dark winter days of late November 1786. The celebrated first – or Kilmarnock – edition of his *Poems, Chiefly in the Scottish Dialect* had been published the previous July and had achieved instant popular success. The volume contained most of the poems for which he is best remembered today, including 'The Holy Fair' and 'The Cottar's Saturday Night'. Robert Heron, writing in June 1797, a year after the poet's death, described how eleven years earlier 'even plough-boys and maid-servants would have gladly bestowed the wages which they earned the most hardly . . . if they might but procure the works of Burns'.[1]

Burns's popularity among the agricultural community should give no cause for surprise, because he spent the vast majority of his life involved in one way or another with farming, and he is frequently described and referred to as the 'ploughman poet'. (One critic, following the publication of the *Poems*, dubbed him the 'Heaven-taught ploughman'.)

Burns was born in January 1759 in a long low cottage (the 'auld clay biggin') with a thatched roof at Alloway, then a rural village but now on the southern fringe of Ayr. At the age of seven he moved with his family to Mount Oliphant, a farm to the south-east of Alloway. The poet's brother, Gilbert, wrote later that 'at the age of thirteen [Robert] assisted in threshing the crop of corn, and at fifteen was the principal labourer of the farm . . . I doubt not but the hard labour of this period of his life was in great measure the cause of that depression of spirits with which Robert was so often afflicted through his whole life afterwards.'[2] On a happier note, however, Burns composed his first known song while living at Mount Oliphant. In 1773, aged fourteen and inspired by Nelly Kilpatrick, who was the boy's companion in the harvest field during that autumn, Burns wrote the words of 'Handsome Nell'. Recalling that time ten years later in his *First Commonplace Book*, he explained that 'I never had the least thought or inclination of turning poet till I once got heartily in love, and then rhyme and song were, in a manner, the spontaneous language of my heart.'[3]

Unable to make ends meet on the seventy-odd acres of Mount Oliphant, the family moved again in 1777 to Lochlea Farm to the north-east of Tarbolton, where they stayed for seven years until the poet's father died in 1784. By the time he arrived in Edinburgh, Burns had entered into a partnership with his brother at Mossgiel, near Mauchline; but the relentless hardship of farming in his native Ayrshire, coupled with a particularly turbulent period in his always convoluted love life, had made him give serious consideration to the possibility of emigrating to the West Indies. Now, with those plans abandoned, he had come to Edinburgh intent on finding a publisher who would be prepared to bring out a second edition of his *Poems*.

The journey from Ayrshire to Edinburgh, made on horseback, took Burns two days to complete. Legend has it that he arrived in the Scottish capital with no letters of introduction to any likely patrons and with very few pennies to rub together. He must surely have wondered, as he made his way from home across country, what lay in store for him once he reached his destination. He is said to have met with more than one person en route who was already familiar with his poems, something that undoubtedly would have given him encouragement and massaged his ego into the bargain. However, nobody, least of all Burns himself, could have anticipated the welcome he was actually about to receive.

On his arrival in Edinburgh, Burns made his way to a boarding house in Baxter's Close off the Lawnmarket (the property disappeared long ago) where John Richmond, a friend from Mauchline, was then lodging and where the poet was assured of a ready welcome. The accommodation was humble enough – the pair were even forced to share the room's one bed, and the upper floors of the house served as a brothel – but at least it suited Burns's meagre pocket. According to one observer at the time, Burns spent his first few days in the city 'wandering about, looking down from Arthur's Seat, surveying the Palace [of Holyroodhouse], gazing at the castle, or contemplating the windows of the booksellers' shops, where he saw all works save the poems of the Ayrshire Ploughman.'[4] But, as another of the poet's early biographers, Robert Chambers, noted, Burns was almost immediately spending his evenings 'with beauty, rank and talent'.[5] Indeed, on 7 December, Burns himself was reporting to his Mauchline friend and patron, the lawyer Gavin Hamilton (and the man, incidentally, to whom he had dedicated the Kilmarnock edition of his *Poems*) that 'For my own affairs, I am in a fair way of becoming as eminent as Thomas à Kempis or John Bunyan, and you may expect henceforth to see my birthday inserted among the wonderful events in the Poor Robin's and Aberdeen Almanacs . . .'[6]

Burns went on to tell Hamilton how he had been taken under the wing of the Earl of Glencairn, a member of the prestigious Caledonian Hunt. 'Through my lord's influence, it is inserted in the records of the Caledonian Hunt that they universally, one and all, subscribe for the second edition.'[7] This was a considerable feather in Burns's cap. Glencairn had already used his influence to bring the poet to the attention of William Creech, then Edinburgh's foremost publisher. Henry Cockburn, whose *Memorials of His Time* (1856) contains tantalising glimpses of Edinburgh's early ninteenth-century literary life, described how Creech's premises stood to the north of St Giles's Cathedral in the former Luckenbooths and 'his windows looked down the High Street; so that his sign, "Creech", above his door was visible down to the head of the Canongate . . . The position of his shop in the very tideway of all our business made it the natural resort of lawyers, authors and all sorts of literary idlers, who were always buzzing about the convenient hive. All who wished to see a poet or a stranger, or to hear the public news . . . or yesterday's occurrence in the Parliament House, or to get the publication of the day or newspapers – all congregated there . . .'[8] Robert Chambers, writing in his *Traditions of Edinburgh* (1824), dubbed it 'the Lounger's Observatory, for seldom was the doorway free of some group of idlers, engaged in surveying and commenting on the crowd in front; Creech himself, with his black silk breeches and powdered head, being ever a conspicuous member of the corps'.[9] Creech was the man who would in due course bring out the second edition of Burns's *Poems*. All that remained was for subscribers to be found who would be willing to buy the copies once they were printed, and members of the Caledonian Hunt would account for at least one hundred of these. (Eventually fifteen hundred subscribers were found, promising to buy almost three thousand copies between them.) The only sour note in the whole enterprise was struck by Creech himself, who was to prove extremely tardy in paying Burns the fee that had been agreed between them for the copyright of the work.

Over half a century before Burns first became acquainted with Creech, a shop above the publisher's premises had been occupied by the poet Allan Ramsay. Born in the Lanarkshire lead-mining village of Leadhills in 1686, Ramsay was the author of a pastoral verse comedy, much admired in its time, called *The Gentle Shepherd* (1725). As a young man he had begun work in

Edinburgh as an apprentice wig-maker, eventually setting up his own business probably in the Grassmarket. However, by the early 1720s he had already become known as a poet (a collected edition of his work was published by subscription in 1721), and he turned from wig-making to bookselling as his occupation. 'For some months he had virtually carried on the two trades concurrently,' explained Oliphant Smeaton in his biography of the poet, *Allan Ramsay* (1896), 'his reputation undoubtedly attracting a large number of customers to his shop to have their wigs dressed by the popular poet of the day.'[10]

Ramsay's bookselling business quickly proved a great success and, in 1725, he also established what was believed to be the first circulating library in Scotland, 'whence', as Chambers quaintly phrased it, 'he diffused plays and other works of fiction among the people of Edinburgh'.[11] Operating from the first storey of the premises in the Luckenbooths (demolished *c.* 1817), where, sixty years later, Creech would occupy the floor below, Ramsay's shop inevitably became something of a magnet for Edinburgh's native and visiting literati. 'Here', explained Chambers, 'Ramsay amused [John Gay, author of *The Beggar's Opera* (1728)] by pointing out to him the chief public characters of the city as they met in the forenoon at the Cross. Here, too, Gay read *The Gentle Shepherd*, and studied the Scottish language, so that upon his return to England he was enabled to make [Alexander] Pope appreciate the beauties of that delightful pastoral.'[12] During the course of a varied literary life, Ramsay also edited a four-volume collection of Scottish songs, *A Tea-Table Miscellany* (1724–37) and a compilation of poetry written before 1600, *The Evergreen* (1724).

Ramsay was, by all accounts, a kind and genial man and the city grew proud of him. 'His squat podgy figure waddling down the High Street on his way to his shop in the Luckenbooths, his head covered with the quaint three-cornered hat of the period,' wrote Smeaton, 'was one of the familiar sights of Edinburgh, to be pointed out to strangers with a pride and affection that never diminished.'[13]

After his death in 1758, Ramsay's achievements were somewhat overshadowed by those of his artist son – also named Allan – who, in 1767, was appointed portrait painter to George III. Ramsay the elder suffered competition from other quarters too, as Chambers noted in 1824. 'The splendid reputation of Burns has eclipsed that of Ramsay so effectively that this pleasing poet, and, upon the whole, amiable and worthy man, is now little regarded.'[14]

Burns was fêted and lionised by academics from the University and by members of the Edinburgh aristocracy and social elite. Professor Josiah Walker, who met the poet frequently at various social gatherings in the city, paints a vivid portrait of the ploughman poet. 'He was plainly but properly dressed, in a style midway between the holiday-costume of a farmer and that of the company with which he now associated. His black hair, without powder, at a time when it was very generally worn, was tied behind, and spread upon his forehead. Upon the whole, from his person, physiognomy and dress, had I met him near a seaport, and been required to guess his condition, I should have probably conjectured him to be the master of a merchant vessel of the most respectable class. In no part of his manner was there the slightest degree of affectation . . .'[15]

Despite his life-long country ways, and lack of native style and breeding, Burns made a universally favourable impression in even the most elevated of Edinburgh's salons and drawing-rooms. 'The attentions he received in town from all ranks and descriptions of persons, were such as would have turned any head but his own',[16] declared Dugald Stewart, Edinburgh University's Professor of Moral Philosophy. 'All the faculties of Burns's mind were, as far as I could judge, equally vigorous. From his conversation, I should have pronounced him to be fitted to excel in whatever walk of ambition he had chosen to exert his abilities.'[17]

Burns's own natural response to his arrival in Edinburgh was, not surprisingly, to write a poem, although, perhaps because of the novelty of the diversions by which he was surrounded, the winter of 1786–7 proved to be a disappointment for him from a creative point of view. Nevertheless, his 'Address to Edinburgh' bubbles over with enthusiasm:

> Edina! Scotia's darling seat!
> All hail thy palaces and tow'rs,
> Where once, beneath a Monarch's feet,
> Sat Legislation's sovereign pow'rs:
> From marking wildly-scattered flow'rs,
> As on the banks of Ayr I stray'd,
> And singing, lone, the lingering hours,
> I shelter in thy honor'd shade.

A portrait of Burns was needed to illustrate the second – or what has become known as the Edinburgh – edition of his *Poems*, and Alexander Nasmyth was commissioned to paint it. The Edinburgh-born artist and the poet were roughly the same age – only a year separated them – and they hit it off immediately. Chambers, in his *Life and Works of Robert Burns* (1851), records how, after each sitting, 'Mr. Nasmyth and the poet would take a ramble together, not infrequently to the King's Park, where Burns delighted to climb Arthur's Seat, and lying on the summit, gaze at its grand panorama of twelve of the principal Scottish counties. Having one night transgressed the rules of sobriety, and sat up till an early hour in the morning, they agreed not to go home at all, but commence an excursion to the Pentland Hills . . . The two friends . . . had a fine morning ramble, and having thus cleared off the effects of their dissipation, came down to Roslin to breakfast.'[18]

An interesting footnote to literary history was written in Edinburgh during that winter of 1786–7. Walter Scott was then a boy of fifteen but, as he recalled in a letter to his son-in-law and biographer John Gibson Lockhart, in 1827, he was once briefly in the same company as Burns, and 'had sense and feeling enough to be much interested in his poetry . . . As it was, I saw him one day at the late venerable Professor Fergusson's, where there were several gentlemen of literary reputation . . . Of course, we youngsters sat silent, looked and listened . . . His conversation expressed perfect self-confidence, without the slightest presumption. Among the men who were the most learned of their time and country, he expressed himself with perfect firmness, but without the least intrusive forwardness . . . I do not remember any part of his conversation distinctly enough to be quoted, nor did I ever see him again, except in the street, where he did not recognise me . . .'[19]

While staying in Edinburgh Burns acknowledged his debt to a fellow-poet, Robert Fergusson, the style of whose vernacular poetry he claimed had influenced his own writing. Born in Edinburgh's long since demolished (and malodorous) Cap-and-Feather Close in 1750, Fergusson was the author of 'Leith Races' and many other poems that took as their theme and portrayed diverse aspects of the everyday life of his native 'Auld Reikie':

> Auld Reikie! Wak o' ilka town
> That Scotland kens beneath the moon;
> Whare couthy chiels at e'ening meet
> Their bizzing craigs and mou's to weet:
> And blythly gar auld Care gae bye
> Wi' blinkit and wi' bleering eye . . .

Always struggling against poverty (and, towards the end of his life, battling with mental illness), Fergusson was employed as a solicitor's clerk until his early death at the age of twenty-four.

Discovering his hero's pauper's grave in the Canongate Kirkyard, Burns immediately sought – and was subsequently given – permission from the kirkyard managers in February 1787 to put up a headstone in memory of his 'elder brother in misfortune/By far my elder brother in the Muses'. Burns's plea, addressed to 'the Honourable the Bailies of the Canongate', conveys the strength of his feeling on the matter. 'I am sorry to be told that the remains of Robert Fergusson, the so justly celebrated Poet, a man whose talents for ages to come will do honour to our Caledonian name, lie in your Churchyard among the ignoble Dead, unnoticed and unknown. Some memorial to direct the steps of the Lovers of Scottish Song, when they wish to shed a tear over the "Narrow House" of the Bard who is no more, is surely a tribute due to Fergusson's memory: a tribute I wish to have the honour of paying . . .'[20]

In due course, Burns composed some suitable lines for the headstone's inscription:

> No sculptured marble here, nor pompous lay,
> No storied urn nor animated bust;
> This simple stone directs pale Scotia's way
> To pay her sorrows o'er the Poet's dust.

Writing in his biography, *Robert Fergusson* (1898), A.B. Grosart suggests that the poet should 'be gratefully remembered for what his vernacular poems did for Robert Burns; for what he did in the nick of time in asserting the worth and dignity and potentiality of his and our mother-tongue; for his naturalness, directness, veracity, simplicity, raciness, humour, sweetness, melody; for his felicitous packing into lines and couplets solid common sense . . . and for sustaining the proud tradition and continuity of Scottish song'.[21]

Others, too, later acknowledged the value of Fergusson's work. 'He died in his acute painful youth,' wrote Robert Louis Stevenson in *Edinburgh: Picturesque Notes* (1878), 'and left the models of the great things that were to come . . .'[22] William Wordsworth lamented that 'Fergusson's early death was a great loss to the poetry of Scotland, and would have been a still greater had he not been followed by his mighty successor, Robert Burns, who as a poet was greatly indebted to his predecessor'.[23] Burns himself wrote of Fergusson:

> With tears I pity thy unhappy fate!
> Why is the bard unpitied by the world,
> Yet has so keen a relish of its pleasures?

The Edinburgh edition of Burns's *Poems* was issued by Creech in late April 1787. In addition to the original titles contained in the Kilmarnock edition, the newly written 'Address to Edinburgh' was included, together with another product of that winter's uncooperative Muse, 'Address to a Haggis':

> Fair fa' your honest, sonsie face,
> Great chieftain o' the puddin-race!
> Aboon them a' ye tak your place,
>   Painch, tripe, or thairm:
> Weel are ye wordy o' a grace
> As lang's my arm.

The main purpose of his visit having now been accomplished, Burns prepared to quit the city without further delay. 'I leave Edinburgh in the course of ten days or a fortnight,' he wrote to an acquaintance on 23 April, 'and after a few pilgrimages over the classic ground of Caledonia . . . I shall return to my rural shades, in all likelihood never more to quit them . . . To the rich, the great, the fashionable, the polite, I have no equivalent to offer; and I am afraid my meteor appearance will by no means entitle me to a settled correspondence with any of you, who are the permanent lights of genius and literature.'[24]

If the publisher Creech had been prompt in settling accounts with Burns, then the poet may well have remained in his 'rural shades' indefinitely. After he had toured through the Border country, the summer of 1787 found Burns back home at Mauchline, where he re-established contact with Jean Armour, the wife from whom he was in effect separated, and who he now swiftly succeeded in making pregnant again (their twins had been born the previous year) before upping sticks and embarking on a protracted tour of the Highlands with his friend Willie Nicol, an Edinburgh schoolmaster. By the end of October Burns was once again back in Edinburgh, lodging with a teaching colleague of Nicol's in St James's Square and intent, above everything else, on extracting from Creech the money he was owed.

Burns did not expect to linger very long in Edinburgh on this occasion, as he had the previous winter, but fate had a double blow in store for him: Creech employed a daunting armoury of tactics in order to delay paying Burns his fee and, while the poet waited impatiently for his money (the not inconsiderable sum in those days of one hundred guineas or so), he became the victim of a coaching accident, during the course of which he injured his leg and was unable to walk. However, while laid up he profitably employed some of his time working on contributions to a project that had truly fired his interest: a series of volumes called the *Scots Musical Museum*, compiled by an Edinburgh engraver called James Johnson, and comprising selections of old Scottish songs and airs. Some of Burns's most familiar and well-loved work – material that he had either written himself, or gathered and revised from diverse sources, and including 'My Love is like a Red, Red Rose' and 'Auld Lang Syne' – appeared in the pages of this extensive collection which was issued between 1787 and 1803.

Having been detained in Edinburgh for much longer than he wished, Burns was chafing at the bit. 'I am here [in St James's Square] under the care of a surgeon,' he wrote to a friend on 12 December, 'with a bruised limb extended on a cushion; and the tints of my mind vying with the livid horror preceding a midnight thunderstorm . . .'[25] However, the unexpected delay was rendered considerably less tiresome for Burns by the fact that, a week or so before writing this letter, he had met Mrs Agnes M'Lehose. She was a young, unhappily married lady in her twenties, and separated from her husband, who was working in the West Indies. When meeting over tea at the house of a mutual friend, Burns and Mrs M'Lehose were instantly attracted to each other and an intense relationship ensued. At first they could only keep in touch by post, owing to the fact that Burns had sustained his accident and was confined to his lodgings for weeks on end before they could arrange to meet again. By the end of December they had still not seen each other for a second time, but they were already signing their letters respectively as 'Clarinda' and 'Sylvander' – 'I like the idea of Arcadian names in a commerce of this kind', declared Burns – and were placing a heavy burden on the postal service between St James's Square and Mrs M'Lehose's home in Potterrow. 'As soon as I can go so far, even in a coach, my first visit shall be to you . . .',[26] the poet promised 'Clarinda'. Meanwhile, he wrote to a friend on the eve of the New Year: 'I am at the moment ready to hang myself for a young Edinburgh widow, who has wit and wisdom more murderously fatal than the assassinating stiletto of the Sicilian bandit, or the poisoned arrow of the African savage.'[27]

By the time Burns was finally able to leave Edinburgh in March 1788 (having received the money he was owed by Creech), 'Clarinda' and 'Sylvander' had notched up a massive correspondence and had even exchanged verses. 'Clarinda' wrote:

> Talk not of love – it gives me pain,
> For love has been my foe:
> He bound me in an iron chain,
> And plunged me deep in woe!

In due course, after revising the words and setting them to an old Scottish tune, Burns was able to include these lines by 'Clarinda' in a volume of the *Scots Musical Museum*.

Meanwhile, anticipating his imminent departure, Burns wrote 'A Farewell to "Clarinda"':

> Clarinda, mistress of my soul,
> The measured time is run!
> The wretch beneath the dreary pole
> So marks his latest sun.

More famously, perhaps, Burns wrote to his 'Fair Empress of the Poet's Soul':

Ae fond kiss, and then we sever!
Ae fareweel, Alas for ever!
Deep in heart-wrung tears I'll pledge thee,
Warring sighs and groans I'll wage thee.

'To understand [Mrs M'Lehose's] friendship with Burns and the meaning of their correspondence, it was almost necessary to have known the woman,' explained Chambers. 'Seeing her and hearing her converse, even in advanced life, one could penetrate the whole mystery very readily, in appreciating a spirit unusually gay, frank and emotional. The perfect innocence of the woman's nature was evident at once; and by her friends it was never doubted.'[28]

However, nothing came of 'Clarinda' and 'Sylvander' beyond a good deal of yearning and sighing. Burns settled down with Jean Armour to the life of a farmer and exciseman in Dumfriesshire. It is to these years that his late masterpiece 'Tam o' Shanter' (1791) belongs. He died at home in Dumfries in 1796 at the relatively young age of thirty-seven. Mrs M'Lehose, on the other hand, survived until 1841, when she died in her native Edinburgh aged eighty-two. She had not seen Burns for half a century, but she never forgot him, and is said to have always kept a portrait of 'Sylvander' with her. Chambers claims that 'to the end of her long life . . . [she] never ceased to bewail his untimely death, and to glow over the productions of his Muse'.[29]

Burns had caught his own measure exactly when describing his brief flowering in Edinburgh's best society as a 'meteor appearance'. To paraphrase Julius Caesar, he came, he saw and he conquered, but when he finally departed there was really only Mrs M'Lehose to mourn his absence. As Michael Schmidt succinctly puts it in his *Lives of the Poets* (1998), 'Literary Edinburgh took him up – no doubt as one who "walked in glory and in joy/Behind his plough", a role he found it hard to sustain without big doses of alcohol and the camaraderie of low types. As a result, literary Edinburgh in general put him down again.'[30]

three

SIR WALTER SCOTT AND HIS OWN ROMANTIC TOWN

S ir Walter Scott's novels enjoyed the kind of popularity during his lifetime and in the years following his death that most authors can only dream about, with the appearance of each new work being an eagerly anticipated event. He was a favourite of other writers too. George Eliot, for example, confided to a friend how she regularly read Scott's novels to her father during the last few years of his life. 'No other writer would serve as a substitute for Scott, and my life at that time would have been much more difficult without him.'[1] Also, the relative merits of his early work were eagerly discussed by Anne Elliot and Captain Benwick, characters in Jane Austen's *Persuasion* (1818).

Scott originally made his mark as a compiler of traditional ballads, with the three-volume *Minstrelsy of the Scottish Border* (1802–3), after which there came a number of major original poetical works, including *The Lay of the Last Minstrel* (1805), *Marmion* (1808) and *The Lady of the Lake* (1810). 'Nobody, not even Scott, anticipated what was to follow,' Henry Cockburn recalled in *Memorials of His Time* (1856). 'Nobody imagined the career that was before him . . . His advances were like the conquests of Napoleon; each new achievement overshadowing the last . . . The quick succession of his original works threw a literary splendour over his native city.'[2]

Scott was born in Edinburgh in August 1771. 'My birth was neither distinguished nor sordid,' he tells us in a fragment of autobiography written in 1808, and which serves as an introduction to the first volume of John Gibson Lockhart's *Life of Sir Walter Scott* (1888 edn). 'According to the prejudices of my country, it was esteemed gentle, as I was connected, though remotely, with ancient families both by my father's and mother's side.'[3] At that time the family lived in a house (long since demolished) in College Wynd off the Cowgate, but it was not long before Scott's parents moved to a more spacious property at 25 George Square (nowadays in the heart of Edinburgh's university quarter) and it was here that he grew up. However, his childhood was punctuated by lengthy absences from home. Aged only eighteen months or so, Scott developed a lameness in his right leg for which various treatments were prescribed and tried out. 'But the advice of my [maternal] grandfather, Dr. Rutherford,' recalled Scott, 'that I should be sent to reside in the country, to give the chance of natural exertion, excited by free air and liberty, was first resorted to; and before I have the recollection of the slightest event, I was . . . an inmate in the farmhouse of Sandy-Knowe [away from the city in the Border country near Kelso] . . . It is here at Sandy-Knowe, in the residence of my paternal grandfather . . . that I have the first consciousness of existence.'[4]

Living in the country did not seem to materially improve Scott's condition, and a few years later he was sent to Bath to 'take the waters'. 'I went through all the usual discipline of the pump-room and baths,' he explained, 'but I believe without the least advantage to my lameness.'[5] However, he did learn to read at a local dame-school, and he was also introduced to the delights of the theatre when a visiting uncle took him to see a production of Shakespeare's *As You Like It*.

Back in Edinburgh, in 1778, Scott became a pupil at the High School where, he reported, 'I did not make any great figure . . . or, at least, any exertions which I made were desultory and little to be depended on.' It was a different story at home, however, where he became a voracious reader and acquired the passion for his country's history and literature that would eventually fuel his own career as a poet and historical novelist. 'In the intervals of my school hours,' he recalled, 'I . . . perused with avidity such books of history or poetry or voyages and travels as chance presented to me – not forgetting the usual, or rather ten times the usual, quantity of fairy tales, eastern stories [and romances].'[6]

Scott left the High School in 1783 and, after spending a few months with an aunt at Kelso in order to build up his strength in the country, he entered Edinburgh University later the same year. He was still only thirteen, but this was the normal practice of the times. Two years later he embarked on a five years' apprenticeship to the legal profession under the direction of his father, who was a Writer to the Signet and – as such – an important figure in Edinburgh's legal circles. Scott described the period of his apprenticeship as 'a dry and barren wilderness of forms and conveyances', but he was eventually called to the Bar in 1792. Thereafter, he pursued a career in the law and made a very handsome living from it, quite apart from any income he derived from his literary endeavours and business interests.

In 1797 Scott married French-born Charlotte Carpenter (or Charpentier) and set up home in a fashionable part of the city, eventually settling with his wife at 39 North Castle Street. But this was only his town house, and he yearned for a country residence too. At first, he rented a cottage at Lasswade, ten miles or so outside Edinburgh. 'In this retreat,' recalled Lockhart, Scott's son-in-law and early biographer, '[the couple] spent some happy summers, receiving the visits of their few chosen friends from the neighbouring city, and wandering at will amidst some of the most romantic scenery that Scotland can boast – Scott's dearest haunt in the days of his boyish ramblings.'[7] In 1804, after he had been appointed Sheriff of Selkirk, Scott took a lease on Ashiestiel, overlooking the River Tweed. 'A more beautiful situation for the residence of a poet could not be conceived,' gushed Lockhart. 'On one side . . . is a deep ravine, clothed with venerable trees, down which a mountain rivulet is heard, more than seen, in its progress to the Tweed . . . and the aspect in every direction is that of perfect pastoral repose.'[8] Eight years later, after buying a small farmhouse with some land beside the Tweed near Melrose, Scott began work on creating his own country mansion and estate, which he called 'Abbotsford'. When he first saw the place, 'the house was small and poor,' explained Lockhart, 'while in front appeared a filthy pond covered with ducks and duckweed, from which the whole tenement had derived the unharmonious designation of "Clarty-Hole" . . . The first hour he took possession he claimed for his farm the name of the adjoining ford . . . As might be guessed from the name of "Abbotsford", these lands had all belonged to the great Abbey of Melrose . . .'[9]

Meanwhile, in Edinburgh Scott pursued his legal career, socialised in the best circles and entertained on a large scale and yet still found time to write. Following the enormous success of his major poems, *Waverley*, the first of his many novels, appeared in 1814 and these continued in a stream of at least one each year until 1831, shortly before his death. The publication of *Waverley*, which was issued anonymously (Scott did not own up to the authorship of his novels until 1827), caused a great stir in Edinburgh's literary circles, according to Cockburn. 'It is curious to remember it. The unexpected newness of the thing, the profusion of original characters, the Scotch language, Scotch scenery, Scotch men and women, the simplicity of the writing, and the graphic force of the descriptions, all struck us with an electric shock of delight . . .

If the concealment of the authorship of the novels was intended to make mystery heighten their effect, it completely succeeded. The speculations and conjectures, and nods and winks, and predictions and assertions were endless, and occupied every company . . .'[10] Most of Scott's fiction, including *Old Mortality* (1816), *Rob Roy* (1817), *The Heart of Midlothian* (1818) and *Redgauntlet* (1824), is deeply rooted in Scotland's turbulent and colourful history.

Everything Scott turned his hand to seemed to flourish – he had also become a partner in the thriving publishing firm of John Ballantyne & Co. – and he rose to become a prominent public figure; his achievements being sealed with the award of a baronetcy in 1818. 'At this moment,' wrote Lockhart, 'his position, take it for all in all, was, I am inclined to believe, what no other man had ever won for himself by the pen alone. His works were the daily food, not only of his countrymen, but of all educated Europe. His society was courted by whatever England could show of eminence. Station, power, wealth, beauty and genius, strove with each other in every demonstration of respect and worship and . . . wherever he appeared, in town or country, whoever had Scotch blood in him, "gentle or simple", felt it move more rapidly through his veins when he was in the presence of Scott.'[11]

Lockhart was certainly able to view Scott's life from a privileged position. Born in Lanarkshire in 1794 and educated at Balliol College, Oxford, he was called to the Scottish Bar (after studying law in Edinburgh) in 1816 and, like his prominent father-in-law – Lockhart married Scott's eldest daughter, Sophia, in 1820 – enjoyed a career that embraced both the legal profession and the city's vibrant literary life. 'In the absence of exact information as to the first half of Lockhart's first year as an advocate,' wrote his biographer Andrew Lang in 1897, 'we may be certain that, like Allan Fairford and Darsie Latimer [characters in Scott's *Redgauntlet*] "he swept the boards of the Parliament House with the skirts of his gown; laughed, and made others laugh, drank claret at Bayle's, Fortune's and Walker's, and ate oysters in the Covenant Close.'"[12]

At the same time, Lockhart also became one of the leading contributors to the city's influential *Blackwood's Magazine*, whose offices in those days could be found on Princes Street. Lockhart served unofficially as the periodical's joint editor for a time, pouring out a stream of erudite and lively articles, including a series of satirical sketches about Edinburgh society which were published by Blackwood in 1819 as *Peter's Letters to his Kinsfolk*.

In 1825 Lockhart moved to London where he went on to edit the *Quarterly Review* for almost thirty years. The frequently waspish tone of his literary criticism inevitably earned him a nickname, 'The Scorpion'. Lockhart also published a handful of now largely forgotten novels, and his *Life of Burns* appeared in 1828, to be followed a decade later by his masterpiece, *Memoirs of the Life of Sir Walter Scott* (1837–8), which ran to seven volumes. Mrs Lockhart thoroughly endorsed her husband's work, telling her father's publisher in the spring of 1836 that '[Lockhart] has read to me, and continues to do so, what he writes, and I am much mistaken if anything in our time will come up to it in interest, style, or as a picture of manners just passing away'.[13] Meanwhile, Lockhart wrote to his father-in-law's old friend and amanuensis, the poet Will Laidlaw, that his 'sole object is to do [Scott] justice, or rather to let him do himself justice, by so contriving it that he shall be as far as possible from first to last, his own historiographer, and I have therefore willingly expended the time that would have sufficed for writing a dozen books on what will be no more than the compilation of one'.[14]

In preparing such a magnificent literary tribute, Lockhart was not simply demonstrating the partiality of a son-in-law for his wife's parent; during his lifetime Scott had made a universally favourable impression, as Cockburn confirms.

'Scarcely . . . even in his novels was he more delightful than in society; where the halting limb, the bur in the throat, the heavy cheeks, the high Goldsmith forehead, the unkempt locks, and general plainness of appearance, with the Scotch accent and stories and sayings, all graced by gaiety, simplicity and kindness, made a combination most worthy of being enjoyed.'[15]

Scott turned 39 North Castle Street into one of Edinburgh's most hospitable addresses. (The house is still standing, but has since been converted from domestic to business premises.) Undeniably one of the greatest figures adorning Edinburgh's legal and literary circles during the first three decades of the nineteenth century, Scott was both a generous and gregarious host whose legendary dinner-parties were given in elegant but at the same time homely and comfortable surroundings. These were occasions when the excellent food vied with sparkling and witty conversation to form the twin attractions for anyone fortunate enough to be invited. But Scott was born of the school that worked hard and played hard, and he often stayed up late into the night, when all was peaceful around him, to write his novels. One of his neighbours at North Castle Street is said to have seen the great man regularly poised over his desk in the candlelight of the small hours long after everyone else had gone to bed.[16]

One of the people who received a ready welcome from Scott in the gracious surroundings of the North Castle Streeet house was the poet and novelist James Hogg, the so-called 'Ettrick Shepherd'. Born the son of a tenant-farmer in 1770, on the banks of Ettrick Water in Selkirkshire, Hogg spent his early life tending cattle and sheep while at the same time attempting to write poetry. Distantly related to Scott's friend Will Laidlaw, he was employed for a decade by Laidlaw's father as a shepherd, before briefly taking over the management of his own father's farm in 1800. The following year, Hogg's debut collection,

Scottish Pastorals, Poems, Songs, etc., was published, and a shared interest in Scotland's native balladry led to his first meeting with Scott in the summer of 1802, at a time when Scott's own *Minstrelsy of the Scottish Border* was making its appearance.

The meeting took place on Hogg's home turf and Scott – whom, as the serving Sheriff of Selkirkshire, Hogg addressed as 'Shirra' – was accompanied by Laidlaw. Hogg was out in the fields when their unexpected approach on horseback was announced. 'I accordingly flung down my hoe,' he recalled, 'and hasted away home to put on my Sunday clothes, but before reaching it I met the "Shirra" and Mr. William Laidlaw coming to visit me. They alighted and remained in our cottage a considerable time, perhaps nearly two hours, and we were friends on the very first exchange of sentiments. It could not be otherwise, for Scott had no duplicity about him; he always said as he thought.'[17]

It was a friendship that would endure until the end of Scott's life – in Hogg, declared Lockhart, 'Scott found a brother poet, a true son of nature and genius hardly conscious of his powers'[18] – and, before long, the 'Ettrick Shepherd' was paying occasional visits to the 'Shirra' in Edinburgh. Lockhart, perhaps unconsciously displaying a trace of 'The Scorpion', describes what happened on one occasion when Scott invited his unsophisticated rustic friend to dinner. 'When Hogg entered the drawing-room Mrs. Scott, being at that time in a delicate state of health, was reclining on a sofa. The Shepherd, after being presented . . . took possession of another sofa . . . and stretched himself thereupon at all his length; for, as he said afterwards, "I thought I could never do wrong to copy the lady of the house" . . . His dress . . . was precisely that in which any ordinary herdsman attends cattle to the market, and his hands, moreover, bore most legible marks of a recent sheep-shearing. The Shepherd . . . dined heartily and drank freely, and, by jest, anecdote and song, afforded plentiful merriment. As the liquor operated his familiarity increased; from Mr. Scott he advanced to "Shirra", and then to "Scott", "Walter" and "Wattie" . . .'[19]

Meanwhile, Hogg's farming fortunes were fluctuating wildly. In 1807 he published a collection of his original ballads, *The Mountain Bard*, and, more prosaically perhaps, a survey of sheep diseases, *The Shepherd's Guide*. With the resulting income, he took the lease on a farm in Dumfriesshire but by 1809 he was bankrupt. Feeling that he had nothing to lose and everything to gain by doing so, Hogg abandoned the farming life and set out for Edinburgh in February 1810, intent on building up his reputation as a man of letters. '[He] had ground for believing that his position in Edinburgh would be, at the worst, not quite so bad as it had now become in Ettrick,' explained Sir George Douglas in his biography, *James Hogg* (1899). 'His published volumes had already won him something of a name; whilst to his literary friends, such as Scott . . . he doubtless felt that he might confidently look for a less sorry reception than awaited him in his native valley. [Having been 'sold up', local farmers were unwilling to employ him.] But with the best will in the world, it is not always possible to befriend budding talent, and the newcomer, who even now, in his own words, "knew no more of human life and manners than a child", must have been grievously disappointed, on reaching the capital, to find his poetical talent rated nearly as low there as his shepherding had been at home. It was in vain that he applied for employment to newsmongers, booksellers and editors of magazines . . .'[20]

However, Hogg did manage eventually to make his mark in Edinburgh's literary circles. He contributed to *Blackwood's Magazine* (he even joined its editorial board) and his long historical sequence of poems, *The Queen's Wake* (1813), sealed his reputation as a poet. Two years later he returned to farming in his native Border country, where he continued to write, but he still visited Edinburgh occasionally, where he had cultivated friends from many walks of life. Robert Chambers describes

how, on the evening before he returned home, Hogg usually
held a farewell dinner, which would be attended by 'meat
dealers . . . from the Grassmarket, genteel and slender young
men from the Parliament House, printers from the Cowgate,
and booksellers from the New Town. Between a couple of young
advocates sits a decent grocer from Bristo Street; and amidst
a host of shop-lads from the Luckenbooths is perched a stiffish
young probationer, who scarcely knows whether he should be
here or not . . . If a representative assembly had been made
up from all classes of the community it could not have been
more miscellaneous than this company, assembled by a man to
whom, in the simplicity of his heart, all company seemed alike
acceptable.'[21] Perhaps Hogg is best remembered today not as a
poet, but for his novel, *The Private Memoirs and Confessions of a
Justified Sinner* (1824), set in early-eighteenth-century Scotland.
His death in 1835 prompted an 'Extempore Effusion' from one
of his admirers, William Wordsworth:

> The mighty Minstrel breathes no longer
> 'Mid mouldering ruins low he lies;
> And death upon the braes of Yarrow,
> Has closed the Shepherd-poet's eyes . . .

Scott shared with Hogg a love of the Borders, and revelled
in the country life of Abbotsford, but he was an Edinburgh
man and proud of his connection with the city. 'Yonder stands
Auld Reekie', declares the falconer in *The Abbot* (1820), when
approaching its outskirts. 'You may see the smoke hover over
her at twenty miles' distance, as the goss-hawk hangs over
a plump of wild ducks – ay, yonder is the heart of Scotland,
and each throb that she gives is felt from the edge of Solway to
Duncan's-bay-head.'[22] And again, his native pride spills out in
this description from *The Heart of Midlothian (1818)*. 'If I were
to choose a spot from which the rising or setting sun could be
seen to the greatest possible advantage, it would be that wild
path winding around the foot of the high belt of semicircular

rocks called Salisbury Crags [in Holyrood Park], and marking the verge of the steep descent which slopes down into the glen on the south-eastern side of Edinburgh . . . When a piece of scenery, so beautiful yet so varied . . . is lighted up by the tints of morning or of evening . . . the effect approaches near to enchantment.'[23]

Lockhart recalls how his father-in-law never seemed happier 'than when placidly surveying, at . . . sunset or moonlit hours, either the massive outlines in his "own romantic town" or the tranquil expanse of its noble estuary. He delighted, too, in passing, when he could, through some of the quaint windings of the ancient city itself . . . How often have I seen him go a long way round about, rather than miss the opportunity of halting for a few minutes on the vacant esplanade of Holyrood, or under the darkest shadows of the Castle Rock, where it overhangs the Grassmarket . . . No funeral hearse crept more leisurely than did his landau up the Canongate or the Cowgate; and not a queer tottering gable but recalled to him some long-buried memory of splendour or bloodshed . . . His image is so associated in my mind with the antiquities of his native place, that I cannot now revisit them without feeling as if I were treading on his gravestone.'[24]

And then, in 1826, Scott's world was turned upside down or, rather, it came crashing down about his ears financially. The cause of his bankruptcy lay far from Edinburgh and largely outside his control. By means of a domino effect that had originated with the partial collapse of the London money market towards the end of 1825, the Edinburgh publishing and printing firm of John Ballantyne & Co., in which Scott owned a third share, went out of business, leaving the author – who had already borrowed heavily from his Abbotsford estate in an attempt to keep the business afloat – with large personal and business debts in excess (it was estimated) of £100,000 and no immediate or visible means of settling with his creditors. Cockburn describes the enormous impact made by this event on Scott's native city. 'The opening of the year 1826 will ever be sad to those who remember the thunderbolt which then fell on Edinburgh in the utterly unexpected bankruptcy of Scott . . . If an earthquake had swallowed half the town, it would not have produced greater astonishment, sorrow, and dismay . . . The idea that his practical sense had so far left him as to have permitted him to dabble in trade, had never crossed our imagination. How humbled we felt when we saw him – the pride of us all, dashed from his honourable and lofty station, and all the fruits of his well-worked talent gone . . .'[25]

Cockburn, who was a contemporary of Scott and for many years leader of the Scottish Bar, was well placed to observe his friend and colleague at close quarters. 'Well do I remember his first appearance after this calamity was divulged, when he walked into Court one day in January 1826. There was no affectation, and no reality, of facing it; no look of indifference or defiance; but the manly and modest air of a gentleman conscious of some folly, but of perfect rectitude, and of most heroic and honourable resolutions. It was on that very day, I believe, that he said a very fine thing. Some of his friends offered him or rather proposed to offer him, enough money, as was supposed, to enable him to arrange with his creditors. He paused for a moment; and then, recollecting his powers, said proudly, "No! This right hand shall work it all off!"'[26]

Writing in the journal that he had begun towards the end of the previous year, Scott records his own brief impressions of that same occasion. 'I went to the Court for the first time today, and like the man with the large nose thought everybody was thinking of me and my mishaps . . . Some smiled as they wished me good day as if to say, "Think nothing about it my lad; it is quite out of our thoughts." Others greeted me with the affected gravity which one sees and despises at a funeral. The best-bred, all I believe meaning equally well, just shook hands and went on . . .'[27]

The journal, which Scott maintained until the end of his life, provides a poignant record of the months immediately following his bankruptcy. Always as good as his word, he set to work straight away in an attempt to pay off all his debts. During the years that followed he produced the novel *Woodstock* (1826), two series of *The Chronicles of the Canongate* (1827 and 1828), a huge biography of Napoleon (1827), *The Tales of a Grandfather* (1827–30) and much else besides. His output was prodigious, and all the more remarkable when measured against the unfortunate change in his circumstances, coupled with the loss of his wife in May 1826.

Because Abbotsford had been settled on his son – also named Walter – a few years earlier, Scott was still able to enjoy the pleasures of the country home which he had created and which was still his pride and joy; but the town house had to be disposed of forthwith. 'This is the first day that a ticket for sale is on my House. Poor No. 39 [North Castle Street],' he wrote on 14 February 1826. 'One gets accustomd [*sic*] even to stone walls and the place suited me very well. All our furniture too is for [sale] – a hundred little articles that seem to me to be connected with all the happier years of my life. It is a sorry business . . .'[28]

Four weeks later, on 15 March, he records: 'This morning I leave . . . Castle Street for the last time . . . I never reckoned upon a change in this particular so long as I held an office in the Court of Session. In all my former changes of residence it was from good to better – this is retrograding. I leave the house for sale and cease to be an Edinburgh citizen in the sense of being a proprietor – which my father and I have been for sixty years at least . . .'[29] From Castle Street, Scott moved into rented accommodation in North St David Street, then Walker Street, before settling for the last few years of his Edinburgh life in lodgings at 6 Shandwick Place, to the west of Princes Street. And during all this upheaval he continued writing at a furious pace to pay off his creditors. 'Corrected proofs and wrote till breakfast. Then the court . . .', he reports on 27 June 1827. 'I set hard to work and had a long day with my new tale,' he writes the following December. 'Worked hard today and only took a half-hour's walk . . .', was one of the next week's entries. 'Another day of labour . . . I worked from eight till three with little intermission,'[30] he lamented the following February. And so it went on. By the time of his death at Abbotsford in September 1832, Scott had not been able to discharge quite all his debts, but nobody could deny that he had made a heroic attempt to do so.

Despite his straitened circumstances, Scott also gradually took up his old place in Edinburgh society once again, where the reversal of his fortunes had not caused anyone to think less of him. 'At select dinner parties, or in other evening gatherings,' wrote David Masson in *Edinburgh Sketches and Memories* (1892), 'he was present again hardly less often than had been his previous custom, – the life of every such company still by his overflowing good humour and endless stock of anecdotes and good stories . . .' Masson goes on to record how Scott was presented with a key to the Princes Street Gardens, which at that time were the private property of those people who resided in Princes Street, 'so that he might walk to and from the Parliament House on a soft velvet turf, amid quiet green shrubbery, and thus lessen the trouble caused by his stiffened joints and the increasing pain of his lameness.'[31] It was appropriate that, a decade or so after Scott's death, a memorial should have been erected to his memory at that spot; a 200-feet-high Gothic spire that has become one of Edinburgh's most distinctive landmarks and which, for anyone prepared to climb the almost three hundred steps to the top, commands a magnificent view over Scott's native city.

—— **four** ——

THOMAS DE QUINCEY
The Mouse in a Blizzard

When the essayist Thomas De Quincey moved to Edinburgh in 1830, he was forty-five years of age, an opium addict with a confirmed literary reputation and, as had been the case throughout his life, struggling desperately to make ends meet. Although not a poet himself, he had been involved for some years with the coterie of 'Lake Poets' centred around the Wordsworths and Grasmere. Having written and published his *Confessions of an English Opium-Eater* De Quincey was, by the late 1820s, spending an increasing amount of his time in Edinburgh, where he had lately become a regular contributor to *Blackwood's Magazine*.

Born in Manchester in 1785, De Quincey was educated first in Bath then later closer to home at Manchester Grammar School, where he was so unhappy that he ran away in July 1802 and lived rough for some time in North Wales. Subsequently, he made his way to London, where he roamed the streets of Soho in a state of near starvation and abject poverty. His circumstances improved considerably the following year, however, when he took up a place at Worcester College, Oxford, to study Greek, Latin and German Philosophy, with the benefit of a comfortable annual allowance from his family. Unfortunately, he left Oxford without taking his degree, having forgotten to attend one of the final examinations!

De Quincey had tried living in Edinburgh on several occasions before eventually making the city his permanent home. The first attempt had come at the end of 1814, but he quickly returned to Grasmere where, having already become an opium addict, he lived on a small family inheritance amid the security of his famous literary friends who resided there.

Six years later De Quincey was once again in Edinburgh, by which time his private income had completely evaporated and he had launched himself on a career in journalism; a path that he would follow until the end of his life. 'De Quincey's second Edinburgh sojourn', wrote Edward Sackville-West in *A Flame in Sunlight* (1936), 'was distinguished by the same social gatherings as the first had been – gatherings at which he did his best to live up to the high standard which he had created for himself on his first visit. But circumstances were inauspicious; he was ill and exhausted, and his brain was struggling painfully under the drug, as under a heavy tarpaulin ...'[1]

De Quincey's 'Confessions' first appeared in *The London Magazine* in 1821 and were published in volume form the following year, thus bringing their author his first taste of literary fame at the comparatively advanced age of thirty-seven. Despite this new-found success, however, De Quincey was persistently dogged by a lack of money and the means to support his wife and young family. In 1817 he had married the daughter of a local farmer in Grasmere; a woman whom the Wordsworths undoubtedly felt was socially inferior to their friend's rank as a 'gentleman'. The marriage caused a chill breeze to waft through the covey of poets, with the inevitable result that De Quincey gradually loosened his ties with the circle that had sheltered him for so long.

De Quincey was drawn to Edinburgh once again when John Wilson, who wrote under the pseudonym 'Christopher North', joined the editorial staff of *Blackwood's Magazine*, and invited his old friend from the Lake District (where Wilson, too, had lived for some years) to contribute to the periodical on a regular basis. In fact, it was at Wilson's house in Gloucester Place that De Quincey stayed, before taking his own lodgings in Great King Street at the end of 1830, once he had been joined in the Scottish capital by his wife and their eight children.

Although De Quincey turned out articles, sketches and miscellaneous pieces of writing at a furious rate (not only for *Blackwood's* but for a variety of other periodicals too), poverty was seldom far away and the wolf sniffed obstinately at his door. The itinerant nature, particularly of his early years in Edinburgh, when he darted from one set of lodgings to another in rapid succession desperately hoping to put his creditors off the scent, could do nothing but increase the heavy burden that was placed on a constitution already severely weakened by years of chronic opium addiction. 'This agonized shifting of a body in pain', wrote Sackville-West, 'was to find its ultimate and most fantastic expression in later years, when De Quincey kept going three or four sets of lodgings in Edinburgh at the same time, spending a week or so in each one of them and moving on when driven out by the spate of books and papers which steadily accumulated.'[2] Forres Street, Princes Street and Duddingston are just a selection of the areas that were 'home' to him at various times.

De Quincey is reputed to have taken advantage on more than one occasion of the ancient privilege of 'sanctuary', offered within the precincts of the Palace of Holyroodhouse, when debts pressed on him more heavily than usual. Imprisonment for debt was not abolished until 1880 (well after De Quincey's lifetime), but before that date a number of sanctuary houses were allocated in the grounds of the Palace to accommodate anyone who might otherwise be liable to incarceration. Mr Chrystal Croftangry, who served as Sir Walter Scott's fictional amanuensis for *The Chronicles of the Canongate*, shared a similar fate with the hapless De Quincey. 'One would think the space sufficiently extensive for a man to stretch his limbs in, as, besides a reasonable proportion of level ground (considering that the scene lies in Scotland), it includes within its precincts the mountain of Arthur's Seat, and the rocks and pasture land called Salisbury Crags. But yet it is inexpressible how, after a certain time had elapsed, I used to long for Sunday [when debtors were allowed their freedom to attend church], which permitted me to extend my walk without limitation. During the other six days of the week I felt a sickness of heart which, but for the speedy approach of the hebdomadal day of liberty, I could hardly have endured. I experienced the impatience of a mastiff, who tugs in vain to extend the limits which his chain permits.'[3]

The overall picture of De Quincey's life in Edinburgh during the 1830s is one of often extreme hardship mixed with no little sadness. Two of his children died in the course of the decade and, in 1837, he also lost his wife. This was a particularly severe blow for him because, despite the controversy and ill-feeling it had engendered in Grasmere twenty years earlier, the marriage had proved to be a most happy one.

Against this bleak background, De Quincey produced a series of articles for *Tait's Edinburgh Magazine* between 1834 and 1840 which, when subsequently collected together in one volume under the title *Recollections of the Lakes and the Lake Poets*, would form the second of the two pillars on which his literary reputation rests today. Like his marriage before them, some of the articles proved to be controversial in Grasmere. De Quincey chose to be not always discreet or charitable about the various members of this once tightly knit group, and rumblings of discontent emerged from the Wordsworths' home at Rydal Mount.

A welcome – and uncharacteristic – measure of stability entered De Quincey's life in 1840 when, with his daughters for company, he took a lease on a cottage then called Mavis Bush (but later renamed De Quincey Cottage) at Polton near Lasswade, about eight miles from the centre of Edinburgh. This was to be his permanent home for the remainder of his life, although work would often take him away from the cottage and back to one of his several sets of lodgings in the city. (For a few years from 1841 he also took rooms in Glasgow, but only stayed in them occasionally when his work made it necessary.)

De Quincey suffered from particularly poor health during much of the 1840s. Almost throughout his life he had been plagued by a gastric complaint; it was a painful condition, and one that had first tempted him to use opium as a means of alleviating the discomfort. Nevertheless, his literary output during this period continued undiminished and he regularly contributed articles and stories to *Blackwood's*, *Tait's*, and the *Edinburgh Review*. His work was distinguished by its erudition, and some of the psychological themes he explored – in *Suspiria de Profundis* (1845), for example, and *The English Mail Coach* (1849), where he dipped his toe in the largely uncharted waters of dreams and their imagery – were somewhat ahead of their time.

One of his Edinburgh friends, J.R. Findlay, has left a vivid account of De Quincey's appearance. 'He was a very little man (about 5 feet 3 or 4 inches); his countenance the most remarkable for its intellectual attractiveness that I have ever seen. His features, though not regular, were aristocratically fine, and an air of delicate breeding pervaded the face. His forehead was unusually high, square and compact. At first sight his face appeared boyishly fresh and smooth, with a sort of hectic glow upon it that contrasted remarkably with the evident appearances of age in the grizzled hair and dim-looking eyes. The flush or bloom on the cheeks was, I have no doubt, an effect of his constant use of opium; and the apparent smoothness of the face disappeared upon examination.'[4] Findlay also mentions De Quincey's 'oddly deferential air' when he was out and about in the Edinburgh streets – perhaps the manner was developed originally as a ruse to avoid the attention of creditors – and how his friend's clothes had 'a look of extreme age, and also of having been made for a person somewhat larger than himself'. Another contemporary observer in Edinburgh confirmed that De Quincey was 'so neglected that he looks like an old beggar, [but] of manners so perfect that they would do honour to a prince, and of conversation un-approached for brilliancy'.[5]

Towards the end of the 1840s, De Quincey took a set of lodgings at 42 Lothian Street (now demolished), and these remained his base for the rest of his days whenever work drew him into the city. It was here that he usually wrote, and where he laboured for many of the last years of his life over a monumental collected edition of his work. Andrew Pennycook includes in his *Literary and Artistic Landmarks of Edinburgh* (1973) a fascinating glimpse of De Quincey given by the following tenant of the same set of rooms: 'The good people of the house, a widow, her maiden sister, and a niece, had a very worshipful recollection of their "nice little gentleman" – that was their phrase for him. They evidently liked him, and said he was "bonnie and soft spoken" . . . This maiden sister seems to have been really a mature guardian angel to De Quincey. More than once she said she had "put him out", when he had fallen asleep with his head on the table, and overturned a candle on his papers . . .'[6]

Meanwhile, at Mavis Bush, where he lived with the surviving members of his dwindling family, he entertained friends and received callers and spent as much of his time as possible. The cottage became a dearly loved retreat for him after an uncomfortably itinerant life. Also, his circumstances had eased to some extent when, after the death of his mother in 1846, he received a steady annual income of £200.

Around 1850, De Quincey was approached by an Edinburgh editor and publisher called James Hogg (not to be confused with the 'Ettrick Shepherd' of the same name), who wanted to issue the definitive collected edition of De Quincey's work. A similar project was already under way in the United States but without De Quincey's involvement. When Hogg first broached the subject, De Quincey was less than enthusiastic. 'Sir, the thing is absolutely, insuperably and for ever impossible,'[7] he declared. After all, nobody knew better than he did the chaotic state of his own archive. Copies (where they existed) of his earlier work languished in odd corners of lodgings all over Edinburgh, as Professor David Masson, who was charged with the task of editing a later edition of the *Collected Works* in the 1880s, explained. 'De Quincey, the feeblest and most helpless of little sexagenarian gentlemen at the time when he was called upon to prepare the collective Edinburgh issue of his writings . . . De Quincey, the shifter in many previous years from lodging to lodging, the burrower even in hiding-holes, each new lodging or hiding-hole plugged in its turn with a chaos of books and papers, amid which the little man sat and worked, ruefully recollecting all the while that he had left unknown deposits of books and papers, in tea-chests and band-boxes, in some of those previous lodgings and hiding-holes, the landladies of which he dared not go near and dreaded visits from – could anyone think it possible that . . . De Quincey should contrive to procure the complete collection of his magazine articles for which Mr. Hogg was waiting?'[8] However, against all odds, Hogg managed to persuade De Quincey to play a full part in producing a collected edition for British readers, and work began in earnest.

'The manner in which De Quincey carried out his work of revision was worthy of a medieaval [*sic*] lunatic asylum,' wrote Sackville-West. 'In the monumental chaos of 42 Lothian Street he could never find any given article, when he happened to want it, and wasted further time in writing to Hogg to explain the delay . . . Wrapt [*sic*] in an old military cloak . . . with tea and laudanum within reach, the harassed little old man would sift, hour after hour, surrounded by indescribable confusion, like a mouse in a blizzard . . . correcting, erasing, adding; substituting one word for another, then impatiently crossing out the substitute and replacing the original word, only to cross that out and replace the substitute once more; appending endless footnotes, and footnotes on footnotes . . .'[9]

Gathering, revising and organising his jumbled papers into a collected edition of his work, one that would eventually run to fourteen volumes (all except the last, which he personally supervised through the press), was a task that occupied De Quincey throughout the 1850s. David Masson, who had met De Quincey on more than one occasion, has left a first-hand impression of him at that time: 'Totally free though he now was from those pecuniary cares which had harassed him the latter part of his life at the Lakes . . . and that long portion of his Edinburgh life which he had now left behind him . . . he was yet the same creature of dark corners, evasive of the element around him, that he had always been. After nearly thirty years of residence in Edinburgh, he still moved about the town, with furtive footsteps, no less the little English alien than he had been when he first came into it by adventure. To the few who had attained to something like intimacy with him, and to whom, in their inexpressible admiration of his abilities and their love of his gentle ways, "an evening with De Quincey" was the highest of possible pleasures, the pleasure was possible only by elaborate stratagem . . . He preferred being shut up by himself all day and every day in Lothian Street, with the variation only of an afternoon ramble still all by himself, through certain purlieus and suburbs . . .'[10]

De Quincey's health declined as the 1850s wore on. During the autumn of 1859 it broke down completely and he died in December at the age of seventy-four. His daughter described how, at the last, De Quincey's 'breathing became slower and slower, and as the world of Edinburgh awoke to busy work and life, all that was mortal of my father fell asleep for ever'.[11] He was buried in St Cuthbert's Churchyard, amid a scene that he would have known well at the west end of Princes Street and below the Castle Rock. Given the life expectancy of the times, and the downright persistence with which he abused his health, De Quincey reached a remarkable age.

———— five ————

THOMAS CARLYLE
The Sage of Chelsea

Thomas Carlyle was one of the nineteenth century's most distinguished men of letters. Historian, philosopher, biographer and essayist, by the time of his death in 1881 at 24 Cheyne Row he was affectionately known as 'the Sage of Chelsea'. His major works included a *History of the French Revolution* (1837) and the enormous six-volume biography *Frederick the Great* (1858–65), which reputedly took him fourteen years to complete and which he described himself 'wrestling with . . . as with the ugliest dragon which blotted out all the daylight and the rest of the world to me, till I should get it slain'.[1]

However, these and his other considerable achievements were undreamt of when, in the dreary early winter of November 1809, fourteen-year-old Carlyle left his native village home in rural Dumfriesshire to walk over 80 miles north from Ecclefechan to Edinburgh, where he was about to take up his place at the University. In deference to his age he did not travel alone; a slightly older local boy called Tom Smail made the arduous three-day trek with him. 'How strangely vivid, how remote and wonderful, tinged with the hues of far-off love and sadness, is that journey to me now,' recalled Carlyle more than half a century later during the 1860s, memories that comprised part of his two volumes of *Reminiscences* which were published posthumously in 1881. 'My mother and father walking with me in the dark, frosty November morning, through the village, to set us on our way . . . I hid my sorrow and my weariness, but had abundance of it chequering the mysterious hopes and forecastings of what Edinburgh and the student element would be.'[2]

The two boys arrived in Edinburgh on the third afternoon of their journey and, after obtaining cheap lodgings for themselves in Simon Square, set out together to explore the city. For Carlyle, the son of a country stonemason, Edinburgh was a truly novel experience permeated with exciting new sights and sensations. 'What streets we went through I don't the least recollect; but have some faint image of St. Giles's High Kirk and of the Luckenbooths there, with their strange little ins and outs, and eager old women in miniature shops of combs, shoe-laces and trifles . . .'[3] Then, after they had lingered in Parliament Square, Tom Smail pushed open a door to reveal 'an immense Hall, dimly lighted from the top of the walls . . . and filled with what I thought (exaggeratively) a thousand or two of human creatures; all astir in boundless buzz of talk and simmering about in every direction . . . By degrees I noticed that some were in wig and black gown, some not, but in common clothes, all well-dressed; that here and there on the sides of the Hall, were little thrones with enclosures and steps leading up; red velvet figures sitting in said thrones, and the black-gowned eagerly speaking to them, – Advocates speaking to Judges, as I easily understood.'[4]

Originally destined to enter the Church, Carlyle spent the next four years as a student at Edinburgh University, returning to his family home at Ecclefechan during the holidays and, later, to nearby Mainhill after his father had changed occupation and gone into farming. (The intrepid reader will be rewarded with a few glimpses of Ecclefechan – or 'Entepfuhl' – in Carlyle's partly semi-autobiographical, but to many modern eyes largely impenetrable, *Sartor Resartus*, first issued as a volume in 1838. The author's description of the German university is believed to have its origins in Edinburgh.)

Carlyle eventually left university without taking his degree, and he also abandoned plans to prepare for the ministry in the Church of Scotland. Instead, he went back to Dumfriesshire where he taught mathematics at Annan Academy, before transferring to another teaching post in Kirkcaldy at a higher salary. He employed his time usefully during the school holidays by reading widely in German and English literature; a practice that would influence the future course of his life. He augmented his teacher's salary with various kinds of literary hack work, and began contributing articles to the *Edinburgh Encyclopaedia*. He also translated from the French a book called *Elements of Geometry*, earning a useful fee of fifty pounds in the process.

In 1818 Carlyle was back in Edinburgh intent on studying the law and possibly making it his future profession. He had saved up a small lump sum to live on, and he occasionally earned some extra cash from his freelance literary work. He took lodgings first in Bristo Street and then in Moray Street and, although money was tight and he was sometimes depressed, the city appeared to suit him. 'Edinburgh, with all its drawbacks, is the only scene for me,' he wrote to his brother John in March 1821, adding that 'the air of Arthur's Seat [where he enjoyed lingering on the summit] is pure as a diamond, and the prospect grander than any you ever saw – the blue, majestic, everlasting ocean, with the Fife hills swelling gradually into the Grampians behind; rough crags and precipices at our feet . . . with Edinburgh at their base, clustering proudly over her rugged foundations, and covering with a vapoury mantle the jagged, black, venerable masses of stonework that stretch far and wide, and show like a city in Fairyland . . .'[5]

However, Carlyle's circumstances were vastly improved in 1822 when he was engaged as a private tutor – at the handsome annual salary of £200 – to Arthur and Charles Buller, two boys who lodged in George Square. 'This was a most important thing to me, in the economics and practical departments of my life,' declared Carlyle. 'From the first, I found my Charles the most manageable, intelligent, cheery and altogether welcome and agreeable phenomenon; quite a bit of sunshine in my dreary Edinburgh element . . . Arthur, a two years younger, kept mainly silent, being slightly deaf . . . but I could perceive that he was also a fine little fellow, honest, intelligent and kind; and that apparently I had been altogether much in luck with this didactic adventure.'[6]

The acquisition of these two amenable pupils significantly improved the material quality of Carlyle's life in Edinburgh, as his friend and earliest biographer J.A. Froude explained: 'Carlyle was now at ease in his circumstances . . . he had no more money anxieties. He was living independently in his own rooms . . . His evenings were his own, and he had leisure to do what he pleased. Yet it was not in his nature to be contented. He was full of thoughts which were struggling for expression, and he was beginning that process of ineffectual labour so familiar to every man who has risen to any height in literature, of trying to write something before he knew what that something was to be; of craving to give form to his ideas before those ideas had taken an organic shape . . .'[7]

By this time, Carlyle had already been introduced to his future wife, Jane Baillie Welsh, the daughter of a general practitioner at Haddington in East Lothian. The couple eventually married in 1826 and settled into their first home together at 21 Comely Bank in the north-west of the city. (The house is still in existence, but it is privately owned and not open to the public.) 'In spite of ill health, I reckon myself moderately happy here, much happier than such a fool as I deserves to be,' Carlyle wrote to a friend soon after moving into Comely Bank.

'My good wife exceeds all my hopes, and is, in truth, I believe, among the best women that the world contains . . . Of society in this Modern Athens, we have no want, but rather a superabundance; which, however, we are fast and successfully reducing down to the fit measure.' More than that, Carlyle seemed content simply to be at home with Jane. 'Round our own hearth is society enough, with a blessing . . . and many a still evening, when I stand in our little flower-garden . . . and smoke my pipe in peace, and look at the reflection of the distant city lamps, and hear the faint murmur of its tumult, I feel no little pleasure in the thought of "my own four walls" and what they hold . . .' In old age, however, he looked back on Comely Bank in a different light, believing that 'except for one darling soul, whose heavenly nobleness, then as ever afterwards, shone on me, and should have made the place bright . . . [it] was a gloomy intricate abode . . .'[8]

All thoughts of the law had now been laid to one side, and Carlyle set about making a career from writing. In 1825, his *Life of Schiller* (the German dramatist) had appeared in book form after being serialised in *The London Magazine*, and he had also been commissiond by an Edinburgh publisher to make a translation of Goethe's *Wilhelm Meister*. Meanwhile, the newly married Carlyles' daily pattern at Comely Bank crystallised into a routine that would eventually reach its full maturity (and almost achieve the status of an art form) during their long years together in Chelsea, with Jane presiding over the sundry concerns of the household while at the same time valiantly striving to shield her husband from the everyday irritations of domestic life that played so heavily on his nerves and wreaked havoc with his concentration, rendering it almost impossible for him to write. Noise, it seems, was Carlyle's particular bugbear, as Thea Holme explains in *The Carlyles at Home* (1965), her highly entertaining account of their years in Chelsea. 'Even when they were first married and living at Comely Bank . . . Jane had been obliged to write polite notes requesting the silencing of "an old maid's house-dog and an only son's pet bantam cock".' Later, at Cheyne Row, 'cocks and pianos were his chief enemies. A cock crowing in the small hours woke him instantly; he would thump his bed in his wrath, then jump up and pace the room, waiting furiously for the next crow, which would sometimes drive him out of the house, to walk about the streets till morning.'[9]

Nowadays we celebrate Jane as a literary figure in her own right for the numerous and entertaining letters that flowed from her pen, but her friends and contemporaries knew her best as an accomplished hostess. '[Carlyle's] wife had a genius for small evening entertainments,' recalled Froude, 'little tea parties such as in after days the survivors of us remember in Cheyne Row, over which she presided with a grace all her own, and where wit and humour were to be heard flashing in no other house we ever found or hoped to find. These began in Edinburgh; and no one who has been once at Comely Bank refused a second invitation . . .'[10]

Towards the end of his life, the widowed Carlyle described those gatherings of his early married life at Comely Bank, and the expert manner in which his wife had arranged them on their shoestring budget. 'We had a little tea-party (never did I see a smaller or a frugaller, with the tenth part of the human grace and brightness) once a week . . . ah me, how she knit up all that into a shining thing! . . . Oh, she was noble, very noble, in that early as in all other periods; and she made the ugliest and dullest into something beautiful! I look back on it as if through rain-bows, the bit of sunshine hers, the tears my own.'[11]

If the married life of the Carlyles sailed on equably enough at Comely Bank – or, at least, as harmoniously as the union of a strong-minded woman and a dour man of peevish temperament would allow – the need for money was always pressing, now that Carlyle was no longer acting as tutor to Charles and Arthur Buller. He would have been more secure financially with a profession behind him or a job of some kind to underpin his earnings from writing. Although her husband was more in favour of the plan than was Jane, the decision was taken in 1828 to leave Comely Bank, in fact to leave Edinburgh entirely, and move to Craigenputtoch, a moorland farm in Dumfriesshire that Jane had inherited from her father. Carlyle reasoned that life in the country would be considerably cheaper than in the city and – perhaps most important of all – 'he could go on with his literature and with his life-task generally in the absolute solitude and pure silence of nature . . .'[12]

The Carlyles stayed at Craigenputtoch for six years, before moving to Chelsea in 1834 and settling into the house at Cheyne Row where they would spend the rest of their long married life together. Carlyle had dallied with the possibility of returning to Edinburgh, while lodging in the city for a few months during the winter of 1833 and gathering material for his proposed book about the French Revolution. In the end, however, he decided in favour of a move to London instead. 'As for the people [in Edinburgh] they are very kind,' he reflected, 'and would give us three dinners for one that we can eat, otherwise I must admit them to be rather a barren set of men . . .'[13]

The success of Carlyle's principal works which, in addition to his books about the French Revolution and Frederick the Great, included an edition of Oliver Cromwell's letters and speeches published in 1845, together with an impressive body of miscellaneous prose on social, historical and philosophical matters, meant that he acquired a reputation both at home and abroad as a great thinker and literary figure. Writing in *The Leader* in 1855, George Eliot declared that 'there is hardly a superior or active mind of this generation that has not been modified by Carlyle's writings; there has hardly been an English book written for the last ten or twelve years that would not have been different if Carlyle had not lived.'[14]

Meanwhile, Carlyle himself had long harboured the suspicion that Edinburgh's academic establishment had been slow to recognise and acknowledge his true value. Thus it gave him particular pleasure when, in the spring of 1866, he was installed as the Rector of Edinburgh University. Jane had not been enjoying the best of health and decided not to join her husband on the long and tiring journey north. Her absence from his side when he gave his rectorial address cast a shadow for him over the whole proceedings. 'Monday at Edinburgh was to me the gloomiest chaotic day,' lamented Carlyle in his *Reminiscences*, 'nearly intolerable for confusion, crowding, noisy insanity and misery, – till once I got it done. My speech was delivered as if in a mood of defiant despair, and under the pressure of nightmares . . . The applause etc. I took for empty noise, which it really was not altogether; the instant I found myself loose, I hurried joyfully out of it.'[15] Less than three weeks later, and after forty years of marriage, Jane was dead.

The ownership of Craigenputtoch now fell into Carlyle's hands and, clearly with his own humble and straitened origins in mind, he bequeathed the estate after his death to the University of Edinburgh, so that any income derived from the property could be used to assist students from disadvantaged backgrounds, in the form of the John Welsh bursaries (named in memory of Jane's father). Craigenputtoch itself later reverted to private ownership, while the John Welsh bursaries, as such, ceased to exist twenty or so years ago, when they were amalgamated with other similar awards in a 'streamlining' of competitive bursaries, the general pool of money being used to help students in need and to recognise cases of outstanding achievement.[16]

six

CHARLES DICKENS
Coming Home

Charles Dickens was born in Portsmouth in 1812. The story of his early life – of his impecunious father (who later surfaced in *David Copperfield* thinly disguised as Mr Micawber) and of his unhappy days in the blacking factory off the Strand – has been well documented over the years in countless biographies. However, an overwhelming desire to make something of himself, laced with the awesome capacity for hard work that was to characterise the famous author throughout his adult life, was already present in the young Dickens (who, during his childhood, settled with his family in London). Intent on hauling himself up by his bootstraps, he became a model of self-improvement and, by the age of fifteen, he had started work as an office-boy with a firm of solicitors. He also began to teach himself shorthand and, by his seventeenth birthday, had become a freelance parliamentary reporter, taking down speeches in the House of Commons from a seat in the Gallery. Before long, his reputation for having the fastest and most accurate shorthand of any reporter in London helped to secure him a job – in 1834 – as a young journalist working on the influential London newspaper, the *Morning Chronicle*.

His starting wage of five guineas a week was a decent income for a man of only twenty-two who was without a university education. (One can almost hear Dickens saying that he had been educated in the 'School of Hard Knocks' and the 'University of Life'.) But his job demanded periods of intense concentration and he always worked very long hours, so the money was well deserved.

Dickens had barely got his feet under the table at the *Morning Chronicle* before he was sent north on what was to be the first of many visits to Edinburgh (indeed, it was the most ambitious journey that he had so far undertaken in his young life), to report on a retirement banquet given for the Whig Prime Minister Earl Grey, at which the elderly statesman would also be granted the Freedom of the City. Although the first railway had run between Stockton and Darlington in 1825, the age of the train had still not properly dawned nine years later, so Dickens, accompanied by his friend and fellow reporter Tom Beard, travelled from London by sea to Leith.

Earl Grey's banquet, attended by fifteen hundred or so guests, was held in a specially erected marquee or pavilion on Calton Hill, and Edgar Johnson, writing in *Charles Dickens: His Tragedy and Triumph* (1977 edn), quotes an extract from the reporter's 'copy' for this glittering occasion, published in the *Morning Chronicle* following the event and described by Johnson as 'indubitably pure Dickens'. The report certainly contains more than a hint of the style that would later be employed with such success by the future novelist. Earl Grey and a number of the other principal guests were late in arriving, but one of the diners, apparently unable to curb his appetite, and 'having sat with exemplary patience for some time in the immediate vicinity of cold fowls, roast beef, lobster, and other tempting delicacies [appeared] to think that the best thing he could possibly do would be to eat his dinner while there was anything to eat. He accordingly laid about him with right good-will, the example was contagious, and the clatter of knives and forks became general. Hereupon, several gentlemen, who were not hungry, cried out "Shame!" and looked very indignant; and several gentlemen who were hungry cried "Shame!" too, eating, nevertheless, all the while as fast as they possibly could . . . This is perhaps one of the few instances on record of a dinner having been virtually concluded before it began.'[1]

Dickens was a mere hack, tucked well into the background as an observer on this auspicious occasion but, as Una Pope-Hennessy mused in her biography *Charles Dickens* (1945), 'who among the distinguished guests gathered . . . that evening could have guessed that an insignificant young reporter, at that moment on duty, would in seven years' time be going through the identical experience of Lord Grey in being made a Freeman of the City of Edinburgh?'[2]

In February 1836, on Dickens's twenty-fourth birthday, a collection of his articles and stories that had originally appeared in various periodicals were published in book form under the title *Sketches by Boz* (the pseudonym he had adopted when contributing them). Following the success of this volume, the publishers Chapman and Hall commissioned him to write a serial and, over a period of twenty months from April 1836, *The Pickwick Papers* evolved, appearing in book form in 1837. Dickens the novelist had arrived, and he had not forgotten Edinburgh on the journey. With its loosely constructed plot, *The Pickwick Papers*, woven around the various adventures and calamities which befall members of the Pickwick Club, is brimful with bizarre and entertaining characters, not least the one-eyed Bagman, who is described as 'a story-teller with a roguish expression of fun and good humour'. In the chapter devoted to 'The Story of the Bagman's Uncle', Dickens demonstrates how, during his first visit to Edinburgh a few years earlier, he had already acquired the novelist's gift for storing up impressions that could be put to good use at a later date.

We first encounter the Bagman's uncle in the Canongate. 'On either side of him, there shot up against the dark sky tall gaunt straggling houses with time-stained fronts, and windows that seemed to have shared the lot of eyes in mortals, and to have grown dim and sunken with age. Six, seven, eight storeys high were the houses; storey piled above storey, as children build with cards – throwing their dark shadows over the roughly paved road, and making the dark night darker. A few oil lamps were scattered at long distances, but they only served to mark the dirty entrance to some narrow close, or to show where a common stair communicated, by steep and intricate windings, with various flats above.' After enjoying a most convivial supper at a friend's house, comprising kippered salmon, Finnan haddocks, a lamb's head, a haggis, and many tumblers of whisky, the Bagman's uncle was wending his uncertain way home to Leith Walk, following a route that steered him unsteadily across the North Bridge. 'Here he stopped for a minute, to look at the strange irregular clusters of lights piled one above the other, and twinkling afar off so high, that they looked like stars, gleaming from the castle walls on the one side and the Calton Hill on the other, as if they illuminated veritable castles in the air; while the old picturesque town slept peacefully on, in gloom and darkness below: its palace and chapel of Holyrood, guarded day and night . . . by old Arthur's Seat, towering surly and dark, like some gruff genius, over the ancient city he has watched so long.'[3]

After an initially lukewarm reception, *The Pickwick Papers* caught the public's imagination and propelled Dickens into an immensely successful career as a novelist. By the time of his next visit to Edinburgh, in June 1841, when he was given the Freedom of the City, he had also written *Oliver Twist* (1838), *Nicholas Nickleby* (1839), *The Old Curiosity Shop* (1841), and he was working on *Barnaby Rudge* (1841). This was an astonishingly fertile burst of creative energy from a man who was still only twenty-nine years of age. On hand to see her young husband receive the first great public honour of his career was Dickens's Edinburgh-born wife, Catherine, the eldest daughter of George Hogarth, a music critic, journalist and author who was, boasted Dickens in 1836 shortly before his marriage, 'the most intimate friend and companion of Sir Walter Scott, and one of the most eminent among the literati of Edinburgh'.[4]

The couple installed themselves at the Royal Hotel which was, according to Dickens in a letter to his friend and future biographer John Forster, 'perfectly besieged, and I have been forced to take refuge in a sequestered apartment at the end of a long passage . . . We are very well off in point of rooms . . . The castle is in front of the windows and the view noble.'[5]

A dinner was held in Dickens's honour at the Waterloo Rooms a few days before he was due to formally receive the Freedom of Edinburgh. It was attended by several hundred guests and he was welcomed with hearty enthusiasm. 'The distinction you have conferred upon me', he told his hosts, 'is one I never hoped for and of which I never dared to dream. I thank you again and again with the energy of a thousand thanks in each one.'[6] Dickens was made proud, humble and characteristically emotional by the great outpouring of goodwill shown towards him on this, the first official tribute to his already considerable literary achievements. 'I believe I shall never hear the name of the capital of Scotland without a thrill of gratitude and pleasure,' he declared. 'I shall love while I have life her people, her hills, and her houses, even the very stones of her streets; and if, in the future works which may lie before me, you should discern – God grant you may – a brighter spirit and a clearer wit, I pray you to refer it back to this night, and point to that as a Scottish passage for evermore.'[7] The self-styled 'Inimitable Boz' (he would sometimes refer to himself only half in jest simply as 'the Inimitable') was struck by a rare moment of modesty. 'I felt it was very remarkable', he commented later, 'to see such a number of grey-headed men gathered about my brown flowing locks.'[8]

The dinner had been arranged by one of Edinburgh's most prominent literary and legal figures, Lord Francis Jeffrey, a co-founder of the *Edinburgh Review*. Jeffrey had been in the vanguard of Dickens's Scottish admirers and the two men had struck up a close friendship. Unfortunately, Jeffrey fell ill on the evening in question and Professor John Wilson ('Christopher North'), a leading light on the *Review*'s rival Edinburgh periodical, *Blackwood's Magazine*, presided over the occasion in his place. As a result, we have been left a typically Dickensian sketch of one of Edinburgh's great literary characters. Towards the end of this bibulous evening, Wilson proposed Dickens's health in suitably glowing terms, describing him as a genius who had 'shed a lustre and beauty over paths which before were supposed to be barren and desolate'. Dickens reciprocated by toasting Wilson: 'Who can revert to the literature of the land of Scott and Burns without having directly in his mind . . . that old man of might with his lion heart . . . Christopher North. I am glad to remember the time when I believed him to be a real, actual, veritable old gentleman that might be seen any day hobbling along the High Street with the most brilliant eye and the greyest hair in all the world . . . I had so figured him in my mind; but when I saw the Professor two days ago, striding along the Parliament House, I was disposed to take it as a personal offence. I was vexed to see him look so hearty. I drooped to see twenty Christophers in one.'[9]

These were heady times indeed for Dickens. Still with age, health and seemingly unlimited energy in his favour, he had eclipsed all his contemporaries to become, in a matter of a few years, the most famous and most popular author in the land.

As the 1840s unfolded, Dickens began to diversify. He continued writing, of course; this was the decade that saw the appearance of *A Christmas Carol* (1843), *Martin Chuzzlewit* (1844), *Dombey and Son* (1848), and the first instalments of what was the nearest he ever came to writing an autobiography, *David Copperfield* (1850). However, he

increasingly felt the desire to make personal contact with
his audience in the flesh rather than simply communicating
through the written page. *Nicholas Nickleby* had demonstrated
his affection for the theatre – if Dickens had not been a writer
he might well have become an actor, like his great friend the
tragedian William Charles Macready – and so it is no surprise
that he often threw himself into amateur theatricals. As
one might expect with Dickens, these productions were no
half-hearted affairs. He formed his own amateur company
(mostly comprising friends) in London and took plays out on
tour, donating any proceeds to charity. In 1848, he brought
a production of Shakespeare's *Merry Wives of Windsor* to
Edinburgh's old Theatre Royal in Princes Street, playing the
part of Slender himself. 'The audience, says a contemporary
record, was one of "the most brilliant ever assembled in
Edinburgh"', reported W. Forbes Gray in a 1927 issue of *The
Dickensian*. 'Dickens's Slender, we are told, was "as perfect a
piece of acting as can be seen on the stage."'[10]

It was almost inevitable that, sooner or later, Dickens
would hit upon the idea of performing his own works for his
reading public. The actor in him adored treading the boards
and craved the applause and approval of a 'live' audience. He
always experienced a feeling of profound anti-climax whenever
a tour of his amateur theatricals came to an end. During the
final decade of his life, Dickens travelled the length and breadth
of Britain and toured the United States twice, giving his loyal
and adoring public what amounted to highly charged one-
man shows, rather than simply straightforward readings. He
assumed the part of each different character with gusto, and
invariably proved what a natural and accomplished actor
he truly was. Wherever he appeared he attracted capacity
audiences who were eager, in those days before the advent
of radio and television, to hear the more famous scenes and
characters from his novels brought to life on the stage by the
very person who had created them. Dickens revelled in these

performances, although they eventually placed a heavy burden on his health and undoubtedly hastened his death in 1870 at the early age of fifty-eight.

Dickens gave readings in Edinburgh on at least five occasions, starting with two separate visits in 1858. After the first of these, in March of that year, when he read scenes from *A Christmas Carol* at the city's Music Hall, he confided to the audience that he would never forget or cease to be conscious of the fact that he was 'a burgess and guild brother of the Corporation of Edinburgh. As long as sixteen or seventeen years ago, the first public recognition and encouragement I ever received was bestowed upon me in this generous and magnificent city . . .'[11]

Dickens travelled to Edinburgh again at the end of 1861, on the last date of what had been – as always – a long and exhausting reading tour. He enacted scenes from *The Pickwick Papers* and *Nicholas Nickleby* in the Queen Street Hall, and played to a house so full (because more tickets had been sold for the event than there were seats available) that some members of the audience were obliged to sit on the platform itself. 'Such a pouring of hundreds into a place already full to the throat, such indescribable confusion, such a rending and tearing of dresses, and yet such a scene of good humour, on the whole, I never saw the faintest approach to,' Dickens wrote after the event. 'I read with the platform crammed with people, I got them to lie down upon it, and it was like some impossible tableau or gigantic picnic – one pretty girl in full dress lying on her side all night holding on to one of the legs of my table.'[12]

Dickens's final visit to Edinburgh took place during the early spring of 1869. Despite suffering from increasingly poor health, he had recently devised his most taxing reading to date: the violent scene from *Oliver Twist* in which Bill Sikes murders the hapless Nancy. Predictably, the reading elicited an enormous response from his audience whenever he enacted it. Dickens's old friend Macready, who had been an unrivalled Macbeth in his day, was full of admiration after one such performance in Cheltenham, declaring that it was equal to 'two Macbeths . . . How it is got at, how it is done, how one man can – well! It lays me on my back, and it is of no use talking about it.'[13]

The problem was that each performance of 'Sikes and Nancy' laid Dickens on his back too – literally – and Edinburgh was no exception; not that he ever allowed his poor health to affect a performance. Pope-Hennessy records how, on this occasion after the Edinburgh reading, one member of the audience was so overcome by the proceedings that, according to Dickens, 'he sat staring over a glass of champagne in the wildest way'.[14]

The reading of 'Sikes and Nancy' provided Edinburgh with its last glimpse of the 'Inimitable Boz'. He died in June of the following year after suffering a stroke at his beloved home, Gad's Hill Place, in Kent. Much had happened to him since he first visited Edinburgh as an energetic young reporter on the *Morning Chronicle* in 1834 and, referring again to the early honour that was bestowed on him seven years later by the city fathers, he told the audience who had gathered to hear him read extracts from *A Christmas Carol* at the Music Hall in March 1858, that 'you will readily believe that I have carried . . . through all my subsequent career, the proud and affectionate remembrance of that eventful epoch in my life, and that coming back to Edinburgh is to me like coming home'.[15]

seven

ROBERT LOUIS STEVENSON
A Mind on Fire

'Some men of letters, not necessarily the greatest,' wrote
J.M. Barrie in *An Edinburgh Eleven* (1889), 'have an
indescribable charm to which we give our hearts . . . Of
living authors none perhaps bewitches the reader more than
[Robert Louis] Stevenson, who plays upon words as if they were
a musical instrument . . .'[1] Stevenson was in his late thirties by
this time and had already achieved great fame and popularity
with *Treasure Island* (1883), *The Strange Case of Dr. Jekyll and Mr.
Hyde* (1886) and *Kidnapped* (1886), but literary success had been
carved out against a background of early parental disapproval
and a lifetime of poor health.

Robert Louis Stevenson was born in November 1850 at
Edinburgh's Howard Place but, after an interim move to
nearby Inverleith Terrace, the Stevensons settled in 1857 at
17 Heriot Row, an elegant four-storey Georgian house on the
north side of Queen Street Gardens that would remain their
family home for the next thirty years. Here lived the delicate
young boy who was plagued by bronchial trouble, that

we glimpse in Stevenson's autobiographical poem, 'The Land of Counterpane':

> When I was sick and lay a-bed,
> I had two pillows at my head,
> And all my toys beside me lay
> To keep me happy all the day . . .[2]

Stevenson was born into a family of distinguished engineers. His paternal grandfather, Robert, was responsible for the building of more than twenty lighthouses – including the famous Bell Rock – during his half century with the Northern Lighthouse Board. Stevenson's father, Thomas, followed suit, working as an engineer with the same body. Naturally, perhaps, it was hoped – probably even expected – that Stevenson himself would continue the family tradition, but the young boy's thoughts turned in a different direction. Frequent spells of illness and the resulting periods of enforced solitude set him slightly apart as a child, and helped perhaps to foster his highly developed imagination, his keen interest in everything around him and, above all, his overwhelming desire to express what he felt and saw by writing about it. It was a passion that his family, and in particular his austere father, found difficult to appreciate or understand. 'All through my boyhood and youth I was known and pointed out for the pattern of an idler,' recalled Stevenson, 'and yet I was always busy on my own private end, which was to learn to write. I kept always two books in my pocket, one to read, and one to write in. As I walked, my mind was busy fitting what I saw with appropriate words; when I sat by the roadside, I would either read, or a pencil and a penny version-book would be in my hand, to note down the features of the scene or commemorate some halting stanzas. Thus I lived with words . . . It was not so much that I wished to be an author (though I wished that too) as that I had vowed that I would learn to write . . .'[3] Given this early determination, Stevenson would have been pleased to read how the novelist Eric Linklater viewed his literary style a century later. '[Stevenson] could turn a phrase as neat as a neo-classic scroll, and wrap shrewd comment in it. There was design in his sentences, his paragraphs and his stories. He was conscious, not only of what he had to say, but of how best to say it; and to say what he has to, as well as he can, is a writer's proper courtesy to his readers . . .'[4]

Because of his recurring ill-health, Stevenson's formal schooling in Edinburgh was spasmodic, often interrupted by long periods spent at home in bed and further punctuated by visits abroad in search of a climate that would ease or improve his respiratory condition. Thus his early education was derived from an amalgam of a preparatory school in India Street (off Heriot Row), a private school in Frederick Street, also just a short step from home, and Edinburgh Academy, situated slightly further afield in Henderson Row. To help compensate for his many lost days in the classroom he was also given private tuition, whether he happened to be at home in Edinburgh or travelling abroad with his parents. It is possible to catch a brief but telling glimpse of Stevenson as a young Edinburgh school-boy in this contemporary account of him quoted by Jenni Calder in her biography *R.L.S.: A Life Study* (1980). A fellow pupil described him 'at that time . . . [as] the queerest looking object you could conceive. To begin with he was badly put together, a slithering, loose flail of a fellow, all joints, elbows, and exposed spindle-shanks, his trousers being generally a foot too short in the leg. He was so like a scarecrow that one almost expected him to creak in the wind . . .'[5]

As a delicate child who was often confined to bed, Stevenson was frequently denied the normal rough-and-tumble of boyhood games among companions of his own age, but nevertheless life still held its pleasures. For example, he enjoyed many outings with his young cousins, and in particular one expedition that was repeated time and again as he recalled many years later in an essay, 'A Penny Plain and Twopence Coloured': 'There stands, I fancy, to this day (but now how fallen!) a certain stationer's shop at a corner of the wide thoroughfare that joins the city of my childhood with the sea. When, upon any Saturday, we made a party to behold the ships, we passed that corner; and since in those days I loved a ship as a man loved Burgundy or daybreak, this of itself had been enough to hallow it. But there was more than that. In the Leith Walk window, all the year round, there stood displayed a theatre in working order, with a "forest set", a "combat", and a few "robbers carousing" in the slides; and below and about, dearer tenfold to me, the plays themselves, those budgets of romance, lay tumbled one upon another . . . That shop, which was dark and smelt of Bibles, was a loadstone rock for all that bore the name of boy. They could not pass it by, nor, having entered, leave it . . .'[6]

For the young Stevenson there were two treasured haunts beyond the heart of the city. For many years his maternal grandfather, the Revd Lewis Balfour, was minister of the parish of Colinton and, before his grandfather's death in 1860, Stevenson as a boy spent some happy holidays at the manse in this village which has now been absorbed by Edinburgh's southern suburbs. 'It was a place in that time like no other', explained Stevenson, 'the garden cut into provinces by a great hedge of beech, and overlooked by the church and terrace of the churchyard, where the tombstones were thick, and after nightfall "spunkies" might be seen to dance, at least by children; flower-pots lying warm in sunshine . . . the smell of water rising from all round . . . the sound of water everywhere, and the sound of mills – the wheel and the dam singing their alternate strain; the birds on every bush and from every corner of the overhanging woods pealing out their notes until the air throbbed with them; and in the midst of this the manse.'[7] Here Stevenson paints an idyllic – and no doubt idealised – picture of the country holidays that formed such a pleasant contrast to his childhood life in the city, and during which he would usually have assorted cousins as playmates.

Even better than the manse, though, was the cottage at Swanston, then a village on the fringe of the Pentland Hills but – like Colinton – now part of Edinburgh's outermost southern suburbs. For fourteen years from 1867, Stevenson's father leased Swanston Cottage as a country home for family holidays, and the cottage, the village and the Pentland Hills themselves remained a vital part of Stevenson's 'personal map' for the rest of his life, no matter how far afield his travels took him. His love for Swanston and its surroundings comes flooding out in his novel *St. Ives* (set during the Napoleonic Wars), which remained unfinished at the time of his death in 1894. *St. Ives* was eventually published in 1897, after the novelist and poet Sir Arthur Quiller-Couch had been entrusted with the task of completing it. The eponymous hero (Saint-Yves), a French prisoner of war, manages to escape from Edinburgh Castle where he has been held captive and, for the exigencies of the plot, makes his way out of the city to what is obviously Swanston Cottage. 'It was broad day, but still bitter cold and the sun not up, when I came in view of my destination. A single gable and chimney of the cottage peeped over the shoulder of the hill; not far off, and a trifle higher on the mountain, a tall old white-washed farmhouse stood among the trees, beside a falling brook; beyond were rough hills of pasture . . . The cottage was a little quaint place of many rough-cast gables and grey roofs. It had something the air of a rambling infinitesimal cathedral, the body of it rising in the midst two storeys high, with a steep-pitched roof, and sending out upon all hands . . . one-storeyed and dwarfish projections . . . The place seemed hidden away, being not only concealed in the trees of the garden, but, on the side on which I approached it, buried as high as the eaves by the rising of the ground . . .'[8]

Like any country district, Swanston had its fair share of old characters, and Stevenson treasured them. 'It is impossible,' he wrote of Robert Young the Swanston gardener, 'to separate his spare form and old straw hat from the garden in the lap of the hill, with its rocks overgrown with clematis, its shadowy walks, and the splendid breadth of champaign that one saw from the north-west corner. The garden and gardener seem part and parcel of each other . . .'[9] But Stevenson's particular affection was reserved for John Todd, the Swanston shepherd, 'the oldest herd on the Pentlands [who] had been all his days faithful to that curlew-scattering, sheep-collecting life . . . It was through him that the simple strategy of massing sheep upon a snowy evening . . . was an affair that I never wearied of seeing, and that I never weary of recalling to mind; the shadow of the night darkening on the hills, inscrutable black spots of snow-shower moving here and there like night already come, huddles of yellow sheep and dartings of black dogs upon the snow . . . [and] John winding up the brae, keeping his captain's eye upon all sides, and breaking, ever and again, into a spasm of bellowing that seemed to make the evening bleaker. It is thus that I still see him in my mind's eye . . . his great voice taking hold upon the hills and echoing terror to the lowlands . . .'[10]

Stevenson's first holidays at Swanston coincided with the year during which he entered Edinburgh University. A slight improvement in his health at that time – albeit a temporary one – persuaded him that perhaps he should make an attempt, at least, to follow in his father's and grandfather's footsteps by training to become a civil engineer. Stevenson duly enrolled on the appropriate course, but he knew from the outset that he had made the wrong decision, as his friend the art and literary critic Sidney Colvin explained. 'The mind on fire with its own imaginations, and eager to acquire its own experiences in its own way, does not take kindly to the routine of classes and repetitions . . . According to [Stevenson's] own account he was at college, as he had been at school, an inveterate idler and truant . . .'[11] In 1871, Stevenson's father reluctantly agreed that his son could change courses and read law but, even then, as one fellow student commented, 'we did not look for Louis at . . . lectures except when the weather was bad'.[12] Looking back on his undergraduate self some years later as an entirely different person from the one he had subsequently grown into, Stevenson recalled how 'infinite yawnings during lectures and unquenchable gusto in the delights of truantry [*sic*] made up the sunshine and shadow of [his] college life . . .' On reflection, he was astonished to find 'how much cast down he was at times, and how life (which had not yet begun) seemed to be already at an end, and hope quite dead, and misfortune and dishonour, like physical presences, dogging him as he went'.[13]

Eventually, in July 1875, Stevenson passed his Bar examinations and became an advocate. Shortly afterwards, in a letter to Colvin, he explains that he has pressing bills to settle for a new dress suit and for several new white shirts, 'to live up to my new profession . . . I walk about the Parliament House five forenoons a week, in wig and gown . . .'[14]

However, Stevenson's legal career was short-lived, and the days he spent at Parliament House soliciting for employment as an advocate were few. Having already published essays and articles in a number of periodicals, he was determined to become a professional writer. Within a few years he had produced a couple of travel books based on his own experiences abroad: *An Inland Voyage* (1878) described a tour he had made by canoe through France and Belgium and, the following year, his *Travels with a Donkey in the Cevennes* appeared.

However, in addition to making these excursions further afield, Stevenson also wrote a series of articles – originally published in the periodical *Portfolio* – which, when collected together in volume form at the end of 1878, were called *Edinburgh: Picturesque Notes*. The title is deliberately ironic, because Stevenson was sometimes far from complimentary in these sketches of his native city. Probably nowhere else in his work can we detect more clearly his ambivalent attitude towards the place that nurtured him and to which by birth he belonged; he loved it and loathed it, recording and observing it 'warts and all'. And he was roundly abused by some of his

Edinburgh neighbours for his pains, although, as in this extract about the weather, it is easy to understand why his views sometimes met with local hostility. 'Edinburgh pays cruelly for her high seat in one of the vilest climates under heaven', complains Stevenson. 'She is liable to be beaten upon by all the winds that blow, to be drenched with rain, to be buried in cold sea fogs out of the east, and powdered with the snow as it comes flying southward from the Highland hills. The weather is raw and boisterous in winter, shifty and ungenial in summer, and a downright meteorological purgatory in the spring. The delicate die early, and I, as a survivor, among bleak winds and plumping rain, have been sometimes tempted to envy them their fate. For all who love shelter and the blessings of the sun, who hate dark weather and perpetual tilting against squalls, there could scarcely be found a more unhomely and harassing place of residence . . .'[15]

And again, perhaps reflecting Stevenson's lifelong deep religious differences with his father, and the resulting disharmony between them, he writes: 'Edinburgh is a city of churches, as though it were a place of pilgrimage. Hence that surprising clamour of church bells that suddenly breaks out upon the Sabbath morning from Trinity and the sea-skirts to Morningside on the borders of the hills. I have heard the chimes of Oxford playing their symphony in a golden autumn morning, and beautiful it was to hear. But in Edinburgh all manner of loud bells join, or rather disjoin, in one swelling, brutal babblement of noise. Now one overtakes another, and now lags behind it; now five or six all strike on the pained tympanum at the same punctual instant of time, and make together a dismal chord of discord; and now for a second all seem to have conspired to hold their peace. Indeed, there are not many uproars in this world more dismal than that of the Sabbath bells in Edinburgh . . .'[16] But, as he generously conceded, Edinburgh also had its advantages. 'Into no other city', he wrote, 'does the sight of the country enter so far; if you do not meet a butterfly you shall certainly catch a glimpse of far-away trees on your walk; and the place is full of theatre tricks in the way of scenery. You peep under an arch, you descend stairs that look as if they would land you in a cellar, you turn to the back window of a grimy tenement in a lane – and behold, you are face-to-face with distant and bright prospects. You turn a corner, and there is the sun going down into the Highland hills. You look down an alley, and see ships tacking for the Baltic! . . .'[17]

In 1876, while travelling in France, Stevenson had met Mrs Fanny Osbourne. Despite a considerable age difference between them – Fanny was ten years older than Stevenson – the pair were married in America in 1880, after she had obtained a divorce from her previous husband. The 1880s saw Stevenson continuing to write for a wide range of periodicals, and also establishing himself as a hugely popular novelist. These were the years that witnessed the creation of Long John Silver in *Treasure Island*, of David Balfour and Alan Breck in *Kidnapped* and of the eponymous Dr Jekyll and Mr Hyde. Ravaged as always by ill-health, Stevenson moved to the south coast in 1884, in search of more congenial air for his weak chest and damaged lungs. He lived in Bournemouth for three years before leaving Britain altogether in 1888. He travelled for a while in the South Seas, before eventually settling at Vailima in Samoa, with his wife and family (which now included his widowed mother). He died suddenly in 1894 after suffering a cerebral haemorrhage.

One might imagine that, living on the other side of the world, and at last enjoying better health in a climate that was the antithesis of Edinburgh's, Stevenson would have abandoned all thoughts of his native city, but this was not the case. J.M. Barrie, speaking at a Stevenson Memorial meeting held in Edinburgh in 1896, told his audience about a letter that Stevenson had written from the South Seas to an old friend at home. 'He said he was in a boat as he wrote, and while he had been lying there he had been thinking of his old days at Edinburgh University, the dreams he had dreamt in those days, and how little he had thought at that time that they would be realised . . . and now they had been realised it occurred to him that out of gratitude he might have put at the corner of Lothian Street a tablet in which that little story might be inscribed, so that students who had grown downhearted might perchance look up and be cheered . . .'[18]

Linklater believed that 'no city has had a better expositer than Edinburgh had in Robert Louis Stevenson . . . Suffer though he did, in mind and body, from the chill and rigour of his early life, Stevenson never buttoned and mufflered himself against the fascination of his native place; his fingers may have been white as he wrote, but no one has written of it with a more perceptive or approving eye.'[19] Tangible reminders of Stevenson's presence in and around Edinburgh remain for all to see, not least the long-serving family home in Heriot Row, the manse at Colinton, the cottage at Swanston (although none of these are open to the public), and the Hawes Inn at South Queensferry, which appears in *Kidnapped*. There is also a collection of items relating to his life and work in the city's Lady Stair's House Museum. But, as Claire Harman suggests, in concluding her essay about Stevenson in *Writers and their Houses* (1993), 'a surer way to remember [him] is in the weather that blew him away. It is permanently open to the public, and the best place to find it is on the bridge which connects the Old Town with the New . . . As you lean over, you can recall Stevenson doing just the same, watching the trains steam out of Waverley Station, longing to get away, and longing for home.'[20]

eight

W.E. HENLEY
A Trojan of Letters

Yesterday, Leslie Stephen, who was down here [in Edinburgh] to lecture, called on me and took me up to see a poor fellow, a sort of poet who writes for him, and who has been eighteen months in our infirmary, and may be, for all I know, eighteen months more. It was very sad to see him there, in a little room with two beds, and a couple of sick children in the other bed . . . The poor fellow sat up in his bed with his hair and beard all tangled, and talked as cheerfully as if he had been in a king's palace, or the great King's palace of the blue air . . . I shall try to be of use to him.'[1] Thus wrote Robert Louis Stevenson to a friend in February 1875, after the editor of the *Cornhill Magazine* had introduced him to 25-year-old William Ernest Henley. Henley, the son of a bookseller, was a Gloucester man born in 1849 in the city's Eastgate where he lived for almost half of his life. He is a somewhat shadowy literary figure these days, a familiar name that is hard to place, yet in his time he was a well-known man of letters. (Henley can be glimpsed briefly in the work of Joe Orton. The iconic 1960s' playwright called one of his earliest black comedies *The Ruffian on the Stair*, a title derived from a Henley poem.)

Henley was still a schoolboy when he was first attacked by tuberculosis, a disease that was to pursue him relentlessly over the ensuing years. He lost one foot while in his teens, and it was the search for a cure that eventually drew him away from Gloucester during his early twenties when, in 1873, he became a patient at the old Edinburgh Infirmary, where he was placed under the care of Dr Joseph Lister, the so-called 'father of antiseptic surgery'. Lister's revolutionary treatment of infection had originally met with considerable opposition within the medical profession, but his methods were ultimately vindicated by success and Henley, faced with the imminent possibility of having his remaining foot amputated, believed that Lister was the only doctor in the land who might be able to save it.

Roden Shields, who was one of the two sick children briefly referred to by Stevenson in his letter, recalled Henley's time at Edinburgh Infirmary in an article he wrote for the *Cornhill Magazine*, published in August 1905. 'I was seven years old, and shared my bed with Willie Morrison, a collier's child from Shotts. On the other bed in the little private ward lay W.E. Henley . . . I will only try to give a glimpse of my childhood's association with the tortured Trojan of Letters. All I remember is that . . . he had a plenitude of sandy hair, which, with his rather large front teeth, gave him a fierce aspect. But I had no fear of [him]; we were comrades . . .

'I used to be very curious as to his writing so much, and asked him whom he wrote to. He told me his grandmother. Which reply I thought satisfactory, and considered him an exemplary grandson . . . I used to watch him looking hard at the roof, thinking, smiling, and frowning as if he saw nice things and talked to people. I never dared question him in these moods, but I resolved when I was a man I would get pillows at my back and a desk fitted to my bed, and read and smile and frown like Henley.'[2]

Quite unknown to the young boy in the opposite bed, Henley was spending his time writing and endlessly revising the poems which he would later submit to the *Cornhill* with such great success and which would, in turn, lead to his meeting with Stevenson. Largely born out of his confinement in the infirmary, they included the subsequently much anthologised 'Invictus':

> Out of the black night that covers me
> Black as the pit from pole to pole,
> I thank whatever gods may be
> For my unconquerable soul.
>
> In the fell clutch of circumstance
> I have not winced nor cried aloud;
> Under the bludgeonings of chance
> My head is bloody but unbowed . . .

In the event, it took Lister a full twenty months to save Henley's foot from the knife but, despite the dire circumstances in which he found himself – he described the infirmary as 'half workhouse and half jail' – Henley always kept himself fully occupied, not only by writing poetry but also by teaching himself Spanish, German and Italian.

The last few months of Henley's stay at the infirmary were enlivened by visits from his new-found literary friend. The two men went on occasional outings together, as Stevenson records in a letter written during April 1875. 'My afternoons have been so pleasantly occupied taking Henley drives. I had a business to carry him down the long stair, and more of a business to get him up again, but while he was in the carriage it was splendid. It is now just the top of spring with us . . . You may imagine what it was to a man who has been eighteen months in a hospital ward. The look of his face was wine to me. He plainly has been little in the country before . . .'[3]

Although they came from very different backgrounds, the pair got on together famously, with Stevenson relishing Henley's company and conversation. 'It has been said of him that his presence could be felt in a room you entered blindfold,' recalled Stevenson, 'and . . . there is something boisterous and piratic in [his] manner of talk which suits well enough with this impression. He will roar you down, he will bury his face in his hands, he will undergo passions of revolt and agony . . . [but] . . . throughout, there has been perfect sincerity, perfect intelligence, a desire to hear although not always to listen, and an unaffected eagerness to meet concessions.'[4]

Henley stayed on in Edinburgh for a short time after being discharged from the infirmary, and he managed to obtain some freelance literary work with the Edinburgh-based *Encyclopaedia Britannica*. Later, he moved south to London, where he was appointed the editor of several periodicals, including the influential *Magazine of Art*. Meanwhile, he remained in close touch with Stevenson, and subsequently collaborated with him on the writing of four now largely forgotten plays. The first – and probably the most successful – of the quartet, *Deacon Brodie* (1880), took as its subject the Edinburgh cabinetmaker of that name whose outward respectability masked his nocturnal occupation as an inveterate burglar. 'As the plot was laid in Edinburgh towards the close of the eighteenth century,' explained Kennedy Williamson in his biography *W.E. Henley: A Memoir* (1930), 'the two would no doubt often go . . . and prowl about the wynds and warrens of the old part of the city, getting their minds en rapport with its spirit. Stevenson had an even more concrete link with the ghostly past, for a cabinet made by the Deacon himself had formed part of the furniture of his nursery.'[5]

In 1888, Henley returned to Edinburgh briefly after being appointed as editor of the newly founded *Scots Observer*. 'Accordingly there began to arrive day by day at [his] office at 9 Thistle Street . . . manuscripts of work which Time the Arbiter has placed into the category of classics', recalled Williamson. 'One day in February 1890, Henley picked up a package in an unknown hand. It proved to contain a manuscript headed "Barrack Room Ballads" . . . It is on record that before getting through to the end of it, Henley was flinging himself about and shouting for joy.'[6] Written by Rudyard Kipling, the poems – including 'Danny Deever', 'Mandalay' and 'Gunga Din' – appeared in the *Scots Observer* over a period of several months and today, more than a century later, they still remain high on the list of Kipling's most popular verse.

Henley moved back to London when the *Scots Observer* transferred to the capital under a new name, the *National Observer*, thus bringing to a close his own connection with Edinburgh. Meanwhile, another tie was in the process of breaking. Henley and Stevenson had grown apart, and while specific reasons for their estrangement are hard to find and difficult to fathom, it seems most likely that Mrs Stevenson simply did not share her husband's enjoyment of Henley's company.

By the time of his death in 1903, precipitated by the after-effects of a railway accident, Henley's literary achievements were many and various: poet, playwright, editor, prolific contributor to some of the leading periodicals of his day, and compiler of a seven-volume *Dictionary of Slang*. But perhaps, after all, his greatest claim to fame rests with Stevenson, who readily acknowledged that in creating the character of Long John Silver in *Treasure Island*, he had modelled the one-legged pirate at least to some extent on W.E. Henley, telling his friend on one occasion that 'it was the sight of your maimed strength and masterfulness that begot John Silver'.

— nine —

SIR ARTHUR CONAN DOYLE
Doctor of Detection

Sherlock Holmes must surely be the most famous amateur detective in the world. Twentieth-century crime fiction has certainly given rise to no shortage of rivals – Agatha Christie's Hercule Poirot and Miss Marple, and Dorothy L. Sayers's Lord Peter Wimsey being prominent among them – but Sherlock Holmes, supported by his willing assistant Dr Watson, has remained the doyen of them all ever since he first appeared in *A Study in Scarlet* in 1887. With his trademark pipe and deerstalker hat, together with a plausible London address at 221B Baker Street, Holmes seems to straddle the boundaries of fiction and fact. But, as visitors from all over the world constantly discover to their disappointment, the Baker Street address existed only in Conan Doyle's imagination and had no connection with Holmes outside the realms of fiction. Furthermore, the mental picture of him that many of us carry around probably owes much to the cadaverous features of the late actor Peter Cushing, who portrayed the fictional sleuth – renowned for his daunting powers of deduction and a worrying dependency on cocaine when depressed – in a string of television and film adaptations of the Sherlock Holmes stories.

Sherlock Holmes was the creation of Arthur Conan Doyle, a prolific novelist and author not only of detective stories but of historical and science fiction as well (including *The Lost World* in 1912). He was born on 22 May 1859 in a flat at Picardy Place, a corner of Edinburgh that was so called, he explained in his autobiography, *Memories and Adventures* (1924), 'because in old days a colony of French Huguenots had settled there . . . When I last visited it, it seemed to have degenerated, but at that time the flats were of good repute.'[1] Were Doyle to visit his birthplace now, near the junction of York Place and Leith Walk, he would find that it had been unceremoniously demolished to make way for a roundabout.

Doyle's family on his father's side were artists, and his grandfather, John, built up a considerable reputation for himself in London during the second quarter of the nineteenth century mainly as a caricaturist and cartoonist. Indeed, several of Doyle's uncles enjoyed notable success in various aspects of the art world – one of them became manager of the National Gallery in Dublin – but his father, Charles, despite also being artistically inclined, moved north from London to take a job as a civil servant in Edinburgh, where he was employed as an assistant surveyor in the Board of Works. However, Doyle recalls that the newly established Edinburgh branch of the family was not entirely overlooked by its relations who were living elsewhere. 'When my grandfather's grand London friends passed through Edinburgh they used, to our occasional embarrassment, to call at the little flat "to see how Charles is getting on". In my earliest childhood such a one came, tall, white-haired and affable. I was so young that it seems like a faint dream, and yet it pleases me to think that I have sat on Thackeray's knee.'[2]

Charles would dabble in painting occasionally during his spare time after work but, as Doyle explained, 'it . . . was done spasmodically and the family did not always reap the benefit, for Edinburgh is full of watercolours which he had given away.'[3] All through his life Doyle held the view that his father was the most gifted and original painter in the family, even though these attributes were never to be reflected in commercial success.

Unfulfilled by his job, in which progress and promotion always seemed to elude him, and simply overwhelmed by what Dickens referred to as 'the battle of life', Charles Doyle made a gradual but irreversible descent into alcoholism, and it was against this unenviable domestic background that Mrs Doyle, with some financial help from her wealthier brothers-in-law, decided to send her nine-year-old son Arthur away from home to attend boarding school. Coming from a Roman Catholic family, Doyle was despatched to Hodder in Lancashire, where he spent two years before moving on to Stonyhurst. He set off south with some unhappy memories of Newington Academy, the Edinburgh school 'where a tawse-brandishing schoolmaster of the old type made our young lives miserable. From the age of seven to nine I suffered under this pock-marked, one-eyed rascal who might have stepped from the pages of Dickens.'[4] The regime at Stonyhurst was Spartan and the corporal punishment severe, but no doubt the harsh discipline was better regulated and supervised and more fairly meted out than had been the case at Edinburgh's version of Dotheboys Hall. 'We were all very healthy,' Doyle acknowledged, '[and] we dwelt in a beautiful building, dined in a marble-floored hall with minstrels' gallery, prayed in a lovely church, and generally lived in very choice surroundings . . .'[5]

After leaving Stonyhurst Doyle spent a year at a Jesuit school in Germany, before returning to Edinburgh in 1876 to begin his medical studies. He went back to live with his family who were now residing in Argyle Park Terrace on the edge of the Meadows but whose affairs, he said, were 'still as straitened as ever. No promotion had come to my father, and two younger children . . . had arrived to add to the calls upon my mother.'[6]

The course that Doyle followed in the Faculty of Medicine at the university took him five years to complete. This included an

1. Boyd's Inn (officially called the White Horse Inn), off the Canongate, where Dr James Boswell greeted Johnson on his arrival in Edinburgh in 1773. (James Drummond, 1848.)

2. James's Court, late-nineteenth century, and much altered since Boswell lived here.

3. The Luckenbooths, *c.* 1756, where Creech the publisher had his premises. (Sir Daniel Wilson)

4. Robert Fergusson's headstone in the Canongate Churchyard, erected by Robert Burns in memory of his 'elder brother in misfortune/By far my elder brother in the Muses'.

5. A lantern slide showing the entrance to Baxter's Close, off the Lawnmarket, *c.* 1896, where Burns lodged on first arriving in Edinburgh.

6. 39 North Castle Street, *c.* 1882 (from Grant's *Old & New Edinburgh*). Sir Walter Scott was forced to sell this elegant town house after his bankruptcy.

7. Scott's early rural retreat at Lasswade, near Edinburgh.

8. The Scott Memorial (seen here in the 1920s) remains one of Edinburgh's most distinctive landmarks.

9. Thomas De Quincey's final resting-place in St Cuthbert's Churchyard, below the Castle Rock.

10. De Quincey occasionally fled from his creditors to these sanctuary houses in the shadow of the Palace of Holyroodhouse.

11. The Theatre Royal in Princes Street, 1830, where in 1848 Charles Dickens took the the part of Slender in his own amateur production of *The Merry Wives of Windsor*. (Thomas Shepherd)

12. No. 17 Heriot Row. Robert Louis Stevenson grew up here.

13. Comely Bank, 1910, where the newly-wed Thomas Carlyle and his wife Jane first set up home together. (J. Patrick)

14. Swanston Cottage, *c.* 1905, where Stevenson spent many family summer holidays.

15. A statue of the fictional amateur sleuth Sherlock Holmes stands close to the site of Arthur Conan Doyle's birthplace in Picardy Place.

16. No. 14 Cumberland Street; one of the addresses at which Barrie lodged while a student at the University.

17. Craiglockhart, early twentieth century, the former Hydro turned War Hospital where the poets Wilfred Owen and Siegfried Sassoon met in 1917.

18. The White Hart Inn, Grassmarket, c. 1890, where the Wordsworths lodged in 1803. 'It was not noisy and tolerably cheap,' wrote Dorothy.

19. Tobias Smollett's lodgings in St John Street, pictured here in the 1930s.

20. A quiet corner of Hope Park Square: Rebecca West lived at No. 2.

21. Drummond Place, 1954. Sir Compton Mackenzie lived at No. 31 from 1953 until his death in 1972. (H.D. Wyllie)

22. The Writers' Museum in Lady Stair's Close houses collections relating to Burns, Scott and Stevenson.

23. The slopes of the Pentland Hills, pictured here in the autumn of 2003. This was a favourite haunt of Stevenson and Sassoon.

24. Milne's of Rose Street, one of Edinburgh's 'literary' pubs and celebrated in a poem by Norman MacCaig.

25. Crowds at the entrance tent of the Edinburgh International Book Festival in Charlotte Square Gardens, August 2002.

interruption of one year towards the end of his studies when, in 1880, he spent seven months as the ship's surgeon on board an Arctic whaler called the *Hope*. 'As I was only twenty years of age when I started, and as my knowledge of medicine was that of an average third year's student,' he wrote of the voyage, 'I have often thought that it was as well that there was no very serious call upon my services.'[7]

Doyle was able to pack the work for each academic year into a mere six months, so that he could spend the remainder of his time employed as a medical assistant by various practitioners dotted around the country. This allowed him to earn at least a small amount of money to help support his struggling parents. 'Our family affairs had taken no turn for the better,' he wrote of those days, 'and if it had not been for my excursions and the work of my sisters we could have hardly carried on.'[8]

Looking back on his days as a medical student, Doyle described them as 'one long weary grind'. Edinburgh was a noted centre for medical training at that time and, as Doyle's mother was insistent that he should establish himself in one of the professions, training to become a doctor seemed the most logical step for him to take. He recorded his impressions of the university, employing only a thin veneer of fiction, in his partly autobiographical novel, *The Firm of Girdlestone* (1890): 'Edinburgh University may call herself with grim jocoseness the "alma mater" of her students, but if she be a mother at all she is one of a very heroic and Spartan cast, who conceals her maternal affection with remarkable success . . . The young aspirant pays his pound, and finds himself a student. After that he may do absolutely what he will. There are certain classes going on at certain hours, which he may attend if he choose . . . He may worship the sun, or have a private fetish of his own upon the mantelpiece of his lodgings . . . He may live where he likes, he may keep what hours he chooses, and he is at liberty to break every commandment in the decalogue as long as he behaves himself with some approach to decency within the academical precincts . . .' Elsewhere in the novel Doyle castigates Edinburgh University as 'a great unsympathetic machine, taking in a stream of raw-boned cartilaginous youths at one end, and turning them out at the other end as learned divines, astute lawyers and skilful medical men'.[9]

Although Doyle had chosen to live at home with his parents during his university days, many of his fellow medical students – those who came to study from further afield and could not get home in the evenings, or others whose means allowed them to strike out independently – would have lodged in one of the countless rooming houses that were scattered around the city and which acted as a magnet for penurious undergraduates in search of the cheapest accommodation they could find. Doubtless Doyle visited university friends in their tawdry quarters on more than one occasion, as this detailed vignette of one student's third-floor flat in Howe Street (north of Queen Street Gardens) suggests. 'A dingy sideboard, with four still more dingy chairs and an archaeological sofa, made up the whole of the furniture, with the exception of a circular mahogany centre-table, littered with note-books and papers . . . Along the centre of the sideboard, arranged with suspicious neatness, as though seldom disturbed, stood a line of solemn books . . . Quain's "Anatomy", Kirkes' "Physiology" [etc.] . . . together with a disarticulated human skull. On one side of the fireplace two thigh bones were stacked; on the other a pair of foils . . . and a set of boxing-gloves. On a shelf in a convenient niche was a small stack of general literature, which appeared to have been considerably more thumbed than the works upon medicine.'[10]

Doyle's course included a great deal of medical theory mixed with a certain amount of surgical practice, when students were able to observe surgeons at work in the operating theatre. Although this was undoubtedly invaluable experience, more than one student would have been adversely affected by his first sight of blood, a moment that Doyle captures beautifully in a short story, 'His First Operation', in which a first-year student observes the removal of a tumour from a patient on the operating table in front of him. The surgeon has taken hold of a knife, and is about to make an incision while 'pinching up' the lump between the fingers of his left hand. The hapless student 'tried to think of cricket, of green fields and rippling water . . . of anything rather than of what was going on so near him . . . Minute by minute the giddiness grew more marked, the numb, sickly feeling at his heart more distressing. And then suddenly, with a groan, his head pitching forward and his brow cracking sharply upon the narrow, wooden shelf in front of him, he lay in a dead faint.'[11]

Among those professors whose lectures in botany, chemistry, anatomy and physiology Doyle attended was one man who made a particular impression on the nascent author, and who was destined to become a footnote in literary history. This was Joseph Bell, a surgeon at Edinburgh Infirmary, who was described by Doyle as 'thin, wiry, dark, with a high-nosed acute face, penetrating grey eyes, angular shoulders, and a jerky way of walking'. Bell chose Doyle to assist him as an outpatient clerk, and so the young student was able to observe the master at close quarters. 'He was a very skilful surgeon,' Doyle wrote of him, 'but his strong point was diagnosis, not only of disease, but of occupation and character . . . He often learned more of the patient by a few quick glances than I had done by my questions . . . It is no wonder that after the study of such a character I used and amplified his methods when in later life I tried to build up a scientific detective who solved cases on his own merits and not through the folly of the criminal.'[12] Doyle went on to explain how during one consultation Bell, simply by observing the appearance of the patient in front of him, had deduced that he was a recently discharged non-commissioned officer in a Highland regiment stationed in Barbados. To Bell it was all quite straightforward. The man was Scottish, he possessed an authoritative manner, he was suffering from elephantiasis (which, Bell claimed, was common in the West Indies) and, although polite, the man did not take off his hat (an old army habit) in the surgeon's presence. If he had been out of the service for any length of time he would undoubtedly have done so.

Doyle had already begun writing short stories – and enjoying a small amount of literary success – while he was still a student (he found it to be another useful way of boosting his income), but some years were to elapse before he set his most famous creation, Sherlock Holmes, in front of the reading public. When eventually he did so, some characteristics of the Baker Street detective owed their origins to the Edinburgh professor of Doyle's student days, and to that consultation with the non-commissioned officer in a Highland regiment. Holmes's first words on meeting Dr Watson, in *A Study in Scarlet*, have a distinctly familiar ring to them. 'You have been in Afghanistan I perceive', is his opening remark, and the manner in which he arrives at this conclusion is pure Joseph Bell. 'Here is a gentleman of a medical type, but with the air of a military man. Clearly an army doctor, then. He has just come from the tropics, for his face is dark . . . He has undergone hardship and sickness as his haggard face says clearly. His left arm has been injured . . . Where in the tropics could an English army doctor have seen much hardship and got his arm wounded? Clearly in Afghanistan.'[13] Doyle recalled that Bell 'took a keen interest in these detective tales and even made suggestions which were not, I am bound to say, very practical'.[14]

Doyle graduated from Edinburgh University in 1881 as a Bachelor of Medicine and Master of Surgery, and embarked on his career as a general practitioner. Initially, he established himself at Southsea in Hampshire where, in 1886, he created Sherlock Holmes, although *A Study in Scarlet* did not appear until the following year, when it formed part of *Beeton's Xmas Annual* of 1887. Doyle was paid £25 for the copyright and, he declared, 'never at any time received another penny for it'.

Doyle's connection with Edinburgh had by now virtually drawn to a close, but he returned to the city in 1900 to contest the parliamentary seat of Central Edinburgh in the so-called 'khaki' election held that year in the wake of the Boer War. He stood as a Liberal Unionist and entered the fray with characteristic gusto. By this time, of course, with a succession of Sherlock Holmes stories behind him and many other novels to his name, Doyle was something of a celebrity. Two years later he would be knighted for his support of the British government's policy during the Boer War. 'I spoke from barrels in the street or any other pedestal I could find,' he recalled, 'holding many wayside meetings besides my big meetings in the evenings, which were always crowded and uproarious . . .'[15] In the event he lost the election by a narrow margin, after becoming the target of a last-minute 'smear' campaign organised by an 'Evangelical fanatic' who took exception to the fact that Doyle was a Roman Catholic.

Doyle lived for another thirty years, at first in London and then in Sussex, during which time he was able to give up the medical profession and devote himself entirely to writing and to his increasing preoccupation with spiritualism. In his native city of Edinburgh, a statue of Sherlock Holmes and a simple plaque mark his birthplace.

ten

J.M. BARRIE
Apart from the Crowd

Throughout the 1920s and early 1930s J.M. Barrie, the creator of 'Peter Pan' and then at the height of his fame, rented for six weeks or so every summer the gabled sixteenth-century Stanway House in Gloucestershire. The guests that Barrie drew to this glorious corner of the Cotswolds each year were usually a mixture of family and friends, among whom – until his death in 1930 – could often be found Sir Arthur Conan Doyle. The two men had met as successful writers in London during the 1890s but, quite unknown to either of them in their student days, they had earlier been contemporaries at Edinburgh University. Towards the end of his life Doyle described Barrie as his oldest literary friend, and he was astonished to think that they had never 'brushed elbows . . . in that grey old nest of learning'.

For Sir James Matthew Barrie, Stanway House, together with his permanent home in London's then fashionable Adelphi Terrace, were a far cry from his humble origins at Kirriemuir (now in the Tayside Region), where he had been born the son of a handloom weaver in 1860, and which he called 'Thrums' in the fictionalised and often sentimental accounts of his home town. These stories and novels published under such titles as

Auld Licht Idylls (1888) and *A Window in Thrums* (1889) proved highly popular in their day, and did much to establish his early literary reputation.

The even tenor of Barrie's simple but happy childhood at Kirriemuir was interrupted by a family tragedy, when an older brother David was killed in a skating accident. 'I remember very little about him,' Barrie wrote in *Margaret Ogilvy* (1896), a tender tribute to his mother, 'only that he was a merry-faced boy who ran like a squirrel up a tree and shook the cherries into my lap. When he was thirteen and I was half his age, the terrible news came, and I have been told the face of my mother was awful in its calmness as she set off to get between Death and her boy.'[1] Out of this tragedy, it has often been suggested, emerged a recurring theme of 'the lost boy' that echoed down the years of Barrie's writing and was most famously embraced in *Peter Pan*, the story of the boy who would not grow up, first performed (at the Duke of York's Theatre, London) in December 1904.

Barrie had nursed ambitions to become a writer from his childhood, although 'at twelve or thereabout I put the literary calling to bed for a time, having gone to a school [Dumfries Academy] where cricket and football were more esteemed, but during the year before I went to the university it woke up and I wrote great part of a three-volume novel . . .'[2] He made several half-hearted attempts at the time to have the work published, before quickly realising that it would probably be far better to conceal the manuscript and never let anyone read it. Barrie had been sent south to live with his eldest brother, Alexander, who had recently been appointed to a job as Her Majesty's Inspector of Schools for the district of Dumfries, and had therefore taken a house in the town. Alexander (who was nineteen years older than James) knew that Dumfries Academy was an excellent school, and that his young brother would stand a good chance of obtaining a university place if he became a pupil there.

Barrie returned home at the age of eighteen keen to start work, but his parents wanted him to continue with his education. Unable to resist the gentle pressure that was applied to him, he enrolled as an undergraduate at Edinburgh University towards the end of October 1878.

Initially, Barrie shared lodgings with another student at 14 Cumberland Street before moving on to rooms in 20 Shandwick Place. In the absence of Student Welfare Officers and Halls of Residence, the undergraduates of Barrie's day were left to organise and fend for themselves, as Doyle explained. 'The student lives a free man in his own rooms with no restrictions of any sort. It ruins some and makes strong men of many.'[3] For the poorer students, however (and there were a considerable number of them), the going could be particularly rough. Barrie described their plight in an article that he wrote for the *Nottingham Journal* shortly after leaving Edinburgh. 'I knew three undergraduates who lodged together in a dreary house at the top of a dreary street; two of them used to study until two in the morning, while the third slept. When they shut up their books they awoke number three, who arose, dressed, and studied until breakfast time. Among the many advantages of this arrangement the chief was that, as they were dreadfully poor, one bed did for the three.'[4] Nevertheless, despite this Box and Cox arrangement and the obvious hardships (even the occasional tragedy) endured by these students, Barrie detected an element of nobility in their situation. 'If students occasionally died of hunger . . . and dinners were few and far between, life was still real and earnest; in many cases it did not turn out an empty dream . . .'[5]

Student life was not quite so harsh in Barrie's case as for those he describes in the above extracts. 'Of course it was a life of frugality and economy,' wrote Denis Mackail in *The Story of J.M.B.* (1941), 'almost Spartan, if you like, by modern standards, but to both of these [Barrie] was well used; and there was no sudden glaring contrast in his Edinburgh surroundings to make them seem harder than before. He never had to share a bed or live on a sack of potatoes, he could afford books, newspapers and the theatre, if he were careful, and it hardly sounds like acute penury when we hear of his telegraphing to a Dumfries tailor about the fit of his clothes . . .'[6]

Barrie certainly seems to have fallen on his feet during his last year at university if not before, judging by a letter he wrote in 1920 to his long-standing friend and secretary Lady Cynthia Asquith, who was staying at Grasmere. 'You seem to have got into the hands of the right kind of landlady. She reminds me from your description of a real angel who looked after me in my last year at Edinburgh University, and was loved beyond all words by every student who came under her spell. In after years I used to visit her . . .' (Even in the last few years of his life he helped financially to maintain a memorial to 'my well-loved old landlady Mrs. Edwards'.)[7]

Barrie studied a total of seven subjects at university, including philosophy, metaphysics, Latin and Greek, but he only truly excelled at English literature. Still keen to be a writer, he took a modest – but for him all-important – step towards achieving his aim while at university, by managing to become a freelance theatre critic for one of the city's newspapers, the *Edinburgh Courant*.

The overall impression one gains of Barrie at this time is of a diligent but unexceptional student who, perhaps self-conscious and insecure about his appearance and particularly his lack of height, sometimes kept himself apart from the crowd. There was one student at the university with whom, had the pair ever met during those days, Barrie might have found much in common. (The two men did become acquainted later on.) Samuel Rutherford Crockett had arrived in Edinburgh from his native Galloway in the autumn of 1876. The son of a tenant farmer, he shared lodgings with a cousin – also a student – but felt homesick and uneasy in the big city. 'We lived next to the sky in a many-storied grey house, but one of our two windows . . . looked up to the mural battlements of the Salisbury Crags and across the valley to the western shoulder of Arthur's Seat. That seemed in some far-off way to suggest home. But from the other window, looking down on the twinkling lamps receding into the distances by the city dusk – frankly, to go near them made me giddy.'[8]

Crockett was certainly not one of the poorest students attending the university at that time (he received an annual bursary of twenty pounds although, as he complained, eleven pounds of it was swallowed up by fees) but, on the other hand, he was obliged to supplement his means in order to live reasonably. 'I did journalistic work, my first contributions, paragraph reports, soon being printed in the *Edinburgh Daily Review*. But my earnings were not considerable and I do not think that during my student life in Edinburgh, I ever spent more than nine shillings a week . . . For breakfast and supper we used to have oatmeal porridge; our dinner never exceeded sixpence each. When I was saving up to buy a book I would content myself with a penny roll and a glass of milk.'[9]

Crockett went on to become an extremely prolific novelist of the so-called 'Kailyard School' (a now unfashionable strain of Scottish writing which is usually defined as relying heavily on sentimental portrayals of provincial town life), producing such titles as *The Stickit Minister* (1893) and *Love in Pernicketty Town* (1911), but the popularity of his work has not endured. (During the early years of his career, Barrie himself was also considered a leading member of the 'Kailyard School'.)

Despite his reserved nature, however, Barrie did play a part in some of the university's clubs and activities, including the Debating Society from which he himself admitted that he was once nearly expelled for not paying the fees. But he was undoubtedly lonely, and already suffering from the bouts of depression that would suddenly overwhelm him at unexpected moments throughout the rest of his life, prompting Cynthia Asquith to record at the end of one Stanway summer during the 1930s: 'As always, [Barrie] was fluctuating, unpredictable. Now he would put others on the best possible terms with themselves; now lower the temperature for miles around.'[10]

Robert Galloway, a university contemporary of Barrie's, recalls him as being 'exceedingly shy and diffident . . . I do not remember ever to have seen him either enter or leave a classroom with any companion . . . Yet I remember him distinctly – a sallow-faced, round-shouldered, slight, somewhat delicate-looking figure, who quietly went in and out amongst us, attracting but little observation . . .'[11] We can read Barrie's own view of his young adult self in his volume of autobiography, *The Greenwood Hat* (1937), an odd book 'mellowed in that soft autumn light in which Seventy looks back on Twenty-five'.[12] If this is the Barrie of his immediate post-university years, then it probably tells us much about the recent undergraduate as well. Significantly, perhaps, he refers to himself in the third person, as though he were describing someone else entirely. 'If you could dig deep enough into him you would find first his Rothschildian ambition, which is to earn a pound a day; beneath that is to reach some little niche in literature; but in the marrow you find him vainly weltering to be a favourite of the ladies. All the other cravings he would toss aside for that . . . If they would dislike him or fear him it would be something.'[13]

Barrie graduated from Edinburgh University in 1882 and went home to Kirriemuir. Here, he remembers 'being asked [at that time] by two maiden ladies what I was to be, and when I replied brazenly "An author", they flung up their hands, and one exclaimed reproachfully, "And you an M.A.!"'[14] A decade later, when Barrie was well along the path to success, he could still hardly be described as a prophet in his own country, as Doyle observed when he stayed with Barrie's parents during a Scottish lecture tour in 1893. The townspeople, he discovered, realised that tourists were coming to see the original of 'Thrums' after reading Barrie's books, but at least one local inhabitant was puzzled by this 'inexplicable phenomenon . . . "I suppose you have read them," I said to the wife of the local hotel man. "Aye, I've read them, and steep, steep, weary work it was," said she.'[15] Barrie himself recalled in *Margaret Ogilvy* how 'a devout lady [in Kirriemuir] to whom some friend had presented one of my books, used to say when she was asked how she was getting on with it, "it's dreary, weary uphill work, but I've wrastled through with tougher jobs in my time, and, please God, I'll wrastle through with this one."'[16]

Before long, Barrie was employed by the *Nottingham Journal*, where he was assigned to write leading articles and literary reviews. No doubt his freelance stint as a theatre critic with the *Edinburgh Courant* during his university days stood him in good stead. In the spring of 1885, however, he moved to London where he lost no time in establishing himself as a professional author.

It was in Kensington Gardens, where the 'Peter Pan' statue serves as a reminder of the occasion, that, some time during 1897, Barrie met the two little boys, accompanied by their nurse, who were to inspire the creation of his most enduring character. George, then aged five, and his brother Jack, aged four, were the first of the Davies boys to make Barrie's acquaintance. The story that would take to the stage with such success as *Peter Pan* was initially concocted for their enjoyment alone. 'What was it', wrote Barrie somewhat wistfully in 1928, 'that made us eventually give to the public in the thin form of a play that which had been woven for ourselves alone?' Later, Barrie met the remaining three of the five Davies boys – Peter, Michael and Nicholas – and he always maintained that the character of 'Peter Pan' was a composite of them all. 'I made Peter by rubbing the five of you violently together,' he said, 'as savages with two sticks produce a flame.'[17]

Stevenson had left Edinburgh University three years before Barrie's arrival, and the two men never met, but Barrie clearly wished that it had been otherwise. 'I have no right to be in this volume,' he told Rosaline Masson in 1922, when she invited him to contribute to her book, *I Can Remember Robert Louis Stevenson*, 'but I should like to step into some obscure corner of it so that I may cheer and cheer as the procession of him goes by . . .'[18] Subsequently he wrote to her again: 'I am depressed to read

my own fell admission that I never saw or spoke to R.L.S . . . I
kept hitting my forehead in vain to recall some occasion when I
touched the velvet coat . . . Even without it? Why not?'[19] Barrie
then embarked upon an account of an imaginary meeting with
Stevenson in Edinburgh. It was a longer version, and given in a
slightly different form for the printed page, than a story he related
in person when addressing the Printers' Pension Corporation in
1926, on which occasion he told how the two men had literally
bumped into each other while crossing one of the city's busiest
thoroughfares, Princes Street. Sensing an instant rapport, they
decided to do what would occur to most students who found
themselves in similar circumstances: abandon all present plans,
however urgent, find the nearest pub and have a drink together.
'We went off to a tavern at the foot of Leith Street, where we
drank what [Stevenson] said was the favourite wine of the Three
Musketeers. Each of us wanted to pay, but it did not much matter,
as neither of us had any money. We had to leave the tavern
without [his] velvet coat and without my class books . . .'[20] At the
end of his letter to Miss Masson, Barrie signs off wistfully with the
words, 'Heigho. It might have been.'[21]

By 1909, Barrie was a sufficiently celebrated man of letters
to prompt his old university to award him an honorary degree.
It was the second such mark of recognition to be bestowed on
him, as St Andrews had anticipated Edinburgh by eleven years.
But the praise heaped upon him on this occasion must have
provided some compensation for the delay. 'To speak of the
charm of Mr. Barrie's creations is to speak of what every woman
knows, of what every man knows, and of what every well-bred
child knows . . . The Alma Mater of Scott and Stevenson delights
to reflect that she is also the Alma Mater of Barrie and . . . offers
her highest honour to her illustrious alumnus.'[22] Reporting to
his friend Sylvia Llewelyn Davies in April 1909, Barrie wrote: 'I
am now slowly recovering from the functions, which continued
for about six solid hours . . . The gown turned out to be the
gayest affair, all red and blue . . . Edinburgh is looking at its

best, which I think is the best in the world, for it must be about the most romantic city on the earth. But it strikes cold on me nowadays, for the familiar faces have long been gone and there are only buildings left.'[23]

This was not to be the last of the honours that Edinburgh University conferred on Barrie. In October 1930 he was installed as its Chancellor, in a ceremony of fitting pomp and circumstance. 'Appearance, with immense acclamation of Barrie, as his own, pale, anxious self,' records Mackail. 'Sudden transformation, by means of glorious robes, into a figure of impressive authority and power . . . No jokes this time, and only the most formal reminiscences . . . It's a fine speech, an orator's speech . . . The speech of a real Chancellor, too.'[24]

Although Barrie was now in his seventies and battling against gradually declining health, the Chancellorship brought him back to Edinburgh on a number of occasions during the 1930s to attend various functions in the city. Our last glimpse of him there, however, is a sad one and comes in a letter written to the well-known theatrical manager, C.B. Cochran, from the Caledonian Hotel at the beginning of December 1936, only six months before Barrie's death. A pre-London production of his final play, *The Boy David*, which some commentators believe owes a small subconscious debt – like *Peter Pan* and perhaps *Dear Brutus* (1917) – to the childhood loss of his brother, was under way at the King's Theatre, but Barrie was too ill to take any practical part in the proceedings. 'All going well here but I am not equal to a performance,' he told Cochran.[25] It was the first play Barrie had written for fourteen years, and its mounting on the stage had been much delayed by the serious illness of the leading lady. The play flopped when it later opened in London.

Barrie died in June 1937, and was buried in his home town of Kirriemuir. But, as Mackail records, the university where he had been a student, and whose Chancellor he subsequently became, marked his passing with a service (attended by a large crowd) held within the university precincts at the precise time of his funeral.

eleven

WILFRED OWEN AND SIEGFRIED SASSOON
Passing Bells

Wilfred Owen and Siegfried Sassoon were two of the greatest First World War poets that England produced, and they came from markedly contrasting backgrounds. Owen, the younger of the pair, was born in the north Shropshire market town of Oswestry in 1893, where his father was employed on the railways. Sassoon, on the other hand, was born seven years earlier at Matfield near Tunbridge Wells in Kent, and brought up in the more pampered atmosphere of a well-to-do family. In normal circumstances the two men would probably never have met, and certainly not on anything approaching an equal footing, but war is proverbially a great leveller and, in 1917, 2nd Lieutenant Owen of the Manchester Regiment and his brother officer, 2nd Lieutenant Sassoon of the Royal Sussex Regiment, became friends after both had been admitted as patients at Edinburgh's Craiglockhart War Hospital, standing on the southern outskirts of the city and within a short stride of the Pentland Hills. This military hospital run by the Red Cross, and housed in a dourly forbidding mid-nineteenth-century building which before the war had served as a health-reviving Hydro (more recently it has been in the hands of Edinburgh's Napier University), received officers from the Front who had been sent home suffering from various forms of 'neurasthenia' or, as it was more commonly known at the time and later, 'shell-shock'.

Owen, who arrived at Craiglockhart in the last week of June, was the first of the pair to be admitted. He had been despatched back to Britain having been concussed on the Somme a few months earlier. Following a rigorous examination conducted by an Army Medical Board immediately on his arrival at Southampton (the panel reported that 'there is little abnormality to be observed but he seems to be of a highly-strung temperament'),[1] Owen was sent north to Edinburgh straight away and, early the next morning, he arrived at the city's Waverley station. 'I woke up as we were rounding the coast by Dunbar,' he wrote to his mother. 'I saw nothing waiting to meet me . . . so I went into the hotel and breakfasted hugely. I then walked the lovely length of Princes Street. The castle looked more than ever a hallucination with the morning sun behind it. Or again it had the appearance of a huge canvas scenic device such as surrounds Earl's Court.'[2] After revelling in the atmosphere of an untroubled Edinburgh waking up to just another ordinary day, Owen took a taxi out to Craiglockhart. 'There is nothing very attractive about the place,' he informed his mother. 'It is a decayed Hydro, far too full of officers, some of whom I know.'[3]

Meanwhile, Sassoon's path to Craiglockhart had been a decidedly odd one. Having enlisted in the 1st Battalion of the Sussex Yeomanry in August 1914, at the very beginning of the war, he had been more often than not in the thick of the action for almost three years by the time he arrived at Craiglockhart towards the end of July. Latterly, Sassoon had become increasingly disillusioned with his military masters, and he was so deeply concerned about the course the war was taking – a conflict that was now entering its fourth year – that, in June, he had felt obliged to issue a public Declaration 'as an act of wilful defiance of military authority because I believe that the war is being deliberately prolonged by those who have the power to end it . . . I believe that this war, upon which I entered as a war of defence and liberation, has now become a war of aggression and conquest . . . On behalf of those who are suffering now, I make this protest against the deception which is being practised on them . . .'[4]

This highly controversial act, by a young Army officer who had been awarded the Military Cross for his bravery in action, gained a great deal of attention in the press and even caused rumblings among Honourable Members in the House of Commons. Needless to say the military authorities were deeply embarrassed by the incident. Following examination by a Medical Board, it was concluded that Sassoon was suffering from a mild nervous disorder, and that he would undoubtedly benefit from a stay at Craiglockhart, where he duly arrived on 23 July, almost exactly a month after Owen.

Admission to Craiglockhart was not the outcome that Sassoon had anticipated when issuing his Declaration, but grudgingly he came to realise that it was an improvement on what was at least one of the possible alternatives, bearing in mind that his 'act of wilful defiance' might easily have resulted in a term of imprisonment. 'To be arriving at a shell-shock hospital in a state of unmilitant defiance of military authority was an experience peculiar enough to stimulate my speculations about the immediate future,' he reflected in his fictionalised autobiography, *Sherston's Progress* (1936). 'In the train from Liverpool to Edinburgh I speculated continuously . . . The unhistrionic part of my mind remembered that the neurologist member of my Medical Board had mentioned someone called Rivers. "Rivers will look after you when you get there". I inferred from the way he said it, that to be looked after by Rivers was a stroke of luck for me. Rivers was evidently some sort of great man . . .'[5] So far as the hospital building itself was concerned, it 'had the melancholy atmosphere of a decayed Hydro, redeemed only by its healthy situation and pleasant view of the Pentland Hills,' he recalled, adding darkly that 'by night . . . the hospital became sepulchral and oppressive with saturations of war experience'.[6]

Whereas Sassoon arrived at Craiglockhart as a published poet – his reputation as a war poet, however, would eventually be established by some of the poems included in his collections *The Old Huntsman* (1917) and *Counter-Attack* (1918) – Owen had been writing verse since quite an early age but had not yet appeared in print. He had not even composed most of the poems for which he is now celebrated; these, which owed everything to his experience of war in the trenches, he was just on the threshold of writing. Naturally, however, he was familiar with the work of Craiglockhart's new arrival. 'I have just been reading Siegfried Sassoon, and am feeling at a very high pitch of emotion. Nothing like his trench life sketches has ever been written or will be written,'[7] he told his mother in mid-August. He was somewhat in awe of the older man and his talent, with the result that several weeks were to elapse after Sassoon's arrival before Owen introduced himself. Nearly thirty years after that event, Sassoon described their first meeting in his autobiography, *Siegfried's Journey* (1945): 'One morning . . . there was a gentle knock on the door of my room and a young officer entered. Short, dark-haired, and shyly hesitant, he stood for a moment before coming across to the window, where I was sitting on my bed cleaning my golf clubs. A favourable impression was made by the fact that he had under his arm several copies of *The Old Huntsman*. He had come, he said, hoping that I would be so gracious as to inscribe them for himself and some of his friends. He spoke with a slight stammer, which was no unusual thing in that neurosis-pervaded hospital . . . He had a charming smile, and his manners . . . were modest and ingratiating.'[8]

This initial encounter proved to be a great success and the two men soon became friends. 'He is very tall and stately, with a fine firm chisel'd (how's that) head', Owen wrote to a cousin following that first meeting, adding that 'after leaving him, I wrote something in Sassoon's style . . .'[9] The poem he referred to was called 'The Dead Beat', about a soldier who was in the process of disintegrating physically and mentally amid the horrors of the Front; a man who

> Didn't appear to know a war was on,
> Or see the blasted trench at which he stared . . .

Owen and Sassoon usually met up in each other's rooms during the evening, leaving the daytime free to be occupied in their various and separate ways. There were therapy sessions to be attended with Craiglockhart's doctors (after all, the two men were patients in a 'shell-shock' hospital) but, even so, they were both left with a great deal of spare time on their hands. Owen soon took over the editorship of the hospital magazine, *The Hydra*, and also became one of its most prolific contributors, writing articles, reviews and editorials for the fortnightly issues. He also became an enthusiastic supporter of the Field Club, going on outings with the other members to Edinburgh Zoo or up into the Pentland Hills, attending regular meetings and even – on one occasion – giving a lecture on the topic 'Do Plants Think?'

Harnessing his pre-war experience as a teacher of English in France, Owen devoted some of his time while at Craiglockhart to giving a few lessons a week in English literature at Edinburgh's Tynecastle School. His class of thirty-nine boys was a large one, but he enjoyed teaching them, and his pupils responded so favourably towards him that they made him promise to visit them after he had left Craiglockhart and returned to his regiment. Owen kept his word during a brief weekend visit to Edinburgh while on leave just before Christmas 1917, and was delighted to find that the boys had not forgotten him. 'I went off to Tynecastle,' he informed his mother on 20 December. 'They were in the act of writing Christmas letters to me! My address was on the blackboard, and "original" Christmas cards were all over the room!'[10]

Meanwhile, Sassoon found the atmosphere at Craiglockhart downright oppressive. 'The place was a live museum of war neuroses . . . On the whole, I felt happier outside the hydro than in it, so I went for long walks on the Pentland Hills, which really did seem unaware that there was a war on . . .'[11] Bearing in mind his patient's love of golf and believing that he would benefit mentally from the physical exercise, Sassoon's doctor – and subsequently friend – the noted psychiatrist and neurologist, Dr W.H.R. Rivers, had advised Sassoon to send home for his set of golf clubs, and the suggestion was swiftly acted upon. 'When played seriously, even golf can, I suppose, claim to be "an epitome of human life",' mused Sassoon in *Sherston's Progress.* 'Anyhow, in that fourth October of the war I was a better golfer than I'd ever been before – and, I may add, a better one than I've ever been since. I must admit, though, that I wasn't worrying much about the war when I'd just hit a perfect tee-shot up the charming vista which was the fairway to the first green at Mortonhall . . . [one of] the delightfully unfrequented links which the war had converted into Arcadian solitudes.'[12]

As their friendship blossomed and the two men felt more at ease in each other's company, Owen and Sassoon began to spend some time together away from the confines of Craiglockhart. Jon Stallworthy, writing in his biography *Wilfred Owen* (1974), describes how the pair would sometimes travel out to Milnathort, some distance north of Edinburgh on the opposite side of the Firth of Forth, to spend the evening at a pub called The Thistle. 'Owen [who had taught in Bordeaux before the war] was evidently delighted by the publican's good French name – Dauthieu – and by his wife's good French cooking.

One evening they were invited to dinner, together with two or three other officers and, after their meal, moved into the little parlour where a large Cameron Highlander played the piano and they sang songs of the Bing Boys . . . George Robey, and Ivor Novello's "Keep the Home Fires Burning" . . .'[13]

Back at Craiglockhart, Owen and Sassoon spent many evenings together debating the war and discussing poetry. Following their first meeting, Owen had shown some of his own poems to Sassoon in the hope that the more experienced poet would deliver his opinion of them. Sassoon was in no doubt that the younger man possessed considerable talent but advised him against rushing into print. 'I have an uncomfortable suspicion that I was a bit slow in recognizing the exceptional quality of his poetic gift', confessed Sassoon in *Siegfried's Journey*. 'I was sometimes a little severe on what he showed me, censuring the over luscious writing in his immature pieces . . . It was, however, not until some time in October [1917], when he brought me his splendidly constructed sonnet "Anthem for Doomed Youth", that it dawned on me that my little friend was much more than the promising minor poet that I had hitherto adjudged him to be.'[14]

Owen, delighted by the favourable impression that his recent poems had made on Sassoon, told his mother excitedly on 22 October: 'I wrote quite six poems last week, chiefly in Edinburgh; and when I read them to S.S. over a private tea in his room this afternoon, he came round from his first advice of deferred publishing, and said I must hurry up and get what is ready typed. He and his friends will get [the publisher] Heinemann to produce for me . . .'[15] One of the half dozen poems that Owen referred to was 'Six O'Clock in Princes Street':

> In twos and threes, they have not far to roam,
> Crowds that thread eastward, gay of eyes;
> Those seek no further than their quiet home,
> Wives, walking westward, slow and wise . . .

However, his 'Anthem for Doomed Youth' arguably contains the most famous opening lines of any poem to emerge from the First World War:

> What passing-bells for these who die as cattle?
> Only the monstrous anger of the guns. . .

Sassoon did everything he could to encourage and draw out the poet in Owen during the relatively few months they shared at Craiglockhart. After being passed fit for service at a Medical Board in October, Owen left hospital at the end of that month. Before his departure, as Sassoon recalls in *Siegfried's Journey*, the pair went out for one last meal together in Edinburgh. The evening, which they spent at the Conservative Club in Princes Street (Rivers had engineered the election of Sassoon as an Honorary Member), turned into a hilarious occasion when, 'after a good dinner and a bottle of noble Burgundy had put us in cheerful spirits',[16] the two men laughed endlessly over a book of bad verse that Sassoon had recently received from an aspiring poet.

Owen left Edinburgh by train later that same night, initially returning home to Shropshire before spending much of the winter at Scarborough, on the bracing north-east coast of England. He returned to the Front in the spring of 1918 and was killed in action the following November, within days of the Armistice. Apart from a mere handful, all his poems were published posthumously.

Sassoon remained at Craiglockhart for a month or so after Owen's departure. He was discharged from hospital at the end of November and, following a further interval, rejoined his regiment. But his return to the Front was destined to be of short duration, as he explains in *Sherston's Progress*: 'On February 13th [1918] I had landed in France and again became part of the war machine which needed so much flesh and blood to keep it working. On July 20th the machine automatically returned me to London, and I was most carefully carried into a perfect hospital.'[17] In fact, Sassoon had sustained a head wound and, although the injury was not life-threatening, he was returned to England for the duration and his war, at least, was at an end.

Following the horrors of his years in the trenches, Sassoon went on to enjoy a long life and a fruitful literary career until his death in 1967. After the war poems contained in *The Old Huntsman* and *Counter-Attack*, Sassoon published further volumes of poetry and various prose works, including – in 1948 – a biography of the Victorian novelist George Meredith. However, he achieved lasting success with his evocative, dryly humorous and sometimes poignant semi-autobiographical trilogy which, in addition to *Sherston's Progress*, comprises *Memoirs of a Fox-Hunting Man* (1928) and *Memoirs of an Infantry Officer* (1930).

twelve

AN EDINBURGH REVIEW

The Seventeenth and Eighteenth Centuries

The playwright and poet Ben Jonson had the misfortune to be a contemporary of William Shakespeare, otherwise we might remember him as the foremost dramatist of his age. Even so, a number of his major plays – including *The Alchemist*, *Volpone* and *Bartholomew Fair* – are still regularly performed today, and he was also Britain's first Poet Laureate. On the other hand, the work of Gloucestershire-born John Taylor, the self-styled 'Water Poet' (he was employed for much of his working life as a Thames waterman), has been almost entirely forgotten. But Jonson was one of Taylor's patrons and, when both men found themselves in Edinburgh at the same time during the late summer of 1618, it was inevitable that they should meet. Both had travelled the considerable distance north from London on foot. Jonson, born near the capital but possibly descended from a family who had lived for generations in south-west Scotland, may have felt the same distant call of ancestral voices that draws so many people back to the lands of their forebears nowadays in search of their own roots. While in Edinburgh he was granted the Freedom of the City and also invited to stay with the poet William Drummond of Hawthornden. Drummond wrote an account of Jonson's visit, an occasion which must have had its fair share of awkward moments as this brief extract suggests: '[Jonson] is a great lover and praiser of himself . . . A contemner and scorner of others, given rather to losse a friend than a jest, jealous of every word and action of those about him (especially after drink, which is one of the elements in which he liveth.)'[1]

Taylor's jaunt was of a more purely commercial nature. Before setting out on his journey he had managed to obtain the names of more than fifteen hundred subscribers who were prepared to purchase *The Pennyles Pilgrimage* (1618), an account of his journey from London to Scotland, in which he briefly records his impressions of early seventeenth-century Edinburgh where, descending from the castle, 'I observed the fairest and goodliest streete that ever mine eyes beheld . . . [this was the Lawnmarket, High Street and Canongate] . . . the buildings on each side of the way being all of squared stone, five, six or seven stories high . . . the walles are eight or tenne foote thicke, exceeding strong, not built for a day, a weeke, a month, or a yeare, but from antiquitie to posteritie, for many ages . . .'[2]

In the event, once he returned home many of Taylor's subscribers failed to pay him for their copies of *The Pennyles Pilgrimage*, a fact which made his meeting with Jonson at the playwright's temporary headquarters in Leith all the more timely. 'Now the day before I came from Edenborough I went to Leeth', Taylor records, 'where I found my long approved and assured good friend Master Beniamin Jonson, at one Master John Stuart's House: I thanke him for his great kindnesse towards me; for at my taking leave of him, he gave me a piece of gold of two and twenty shillings to drink his health in England . . . So with a kindly farewell, I left him as well, as I hope never to see him in a worse estate . . .'[3]

Daniel Defoe's name conjures up visions of the shipwrecked Robinson Crusoe and of the ebullient Moll Flanders. The novels which recount the exploits of these characters were written towards the end of Defoe's life, and are probably the two books with which he is most associated today. Yet this butcher's son from London was a prolific author and journalist who turned out scores of books, pamphlets and articles during a long career.

Born in 1660, Defoe was a soldier-adventurer who – more prosaically perhaps – became a hosiery merchant in his native city before seriously establishing himself as a writer in the late 1690s. During the early 1700s he embarked on a series of journeys which carried him the length and breadth of the land, his accounts of which were published later (between 1724 and 1726) as *A Tour through the Whole Island of Great Britain*. It has been suggested that these travels were possibly a by-product of Defoe's role at that time as a government secret agent, a delicate and dangerous position that he filled for more than a decade. However, whatever their underlying purpose might have been, Defoe transformed his excursions into a lively, entertaining and highly informative guide book.

Defoe, like his near-contemporary traveller Celia Fiennes, and William Cobbett a century later, journeyed on horseback, a method of travel that allowed the author ample opportunity to soak up the local atmosphere. He ventured twice into Scotland; no mean feat, perhaps, at an average speed of eight miles per hour and for a Londoner with a decided aversion to mountains and wild places in general.

However, Defoe was determined to be objective. 'Hitherto, all the descriptions of Scotland which have been published in our day, have been written by natives of that country, and that with such an air of the most scandalous partiality, that it has been far from pleasing . . . The world shall, for once, hear what an Englishman shall give of Scotland . . .'[4]

A deeply committed city-dweller at heart, Defoe felt quite at home in Edinburgh, where he marvelled at the wynds and tall buildings and visited the Castle, the Palace of Holyroodhouse and St Giles's Cathedral, just as any average tourist might do today. 'The buildings are surprising . . . for strength, beauty and for height', he declared, 'all, or the greatest part of free-stone, and so firm in everything made, that though in so high a situation, and, in a country where storms and violent winds are so frequent, 'tis very rare that any damage is done here. No blowing of tiles about the streets, to knock people on the head as they pass; no stacks of chimneys and gable-ends of houses falling in to bury the inhabitants in their ruins, as we often find it in London, and other of our paper built cities in England . . .'[5]

Alongside Defoe, Tobias Smollett is regarded as one of the finest early British novelists. Born in Dumbartonshire in 1721, he studied medicine at Glasgow University and joined the Navy as a ship's surgeon, before eventually returning to Britain and settling in London for many years. Towards the end of his life, as his health deteriorated, he spent an increasing amount of his time abroad until his death in 1771. *The Adventures of Roderick Random* (1748) and *The Adventures of Peregrine Pickle* (1751) remain two of his most famous novels, but *The Expedition of Humphry Clinker* (1771) is generally reckoned to be his masterpiece; it was also his last book, published only a few months before he died. Written in the epistolary form popular at that time, it recounts – through a series of letters sent to friends and acquaintances of the characters involved – the wanderings of the irascible and hypochondriac Matthew Bramble. Attended by a party which includes his niece and nephew, Lydia and Jeremy Melford, an elderly unmarried sister Tabitha Bramble, and their maidservant Win Jenkins, he leaves his home in Wales to scour the country in search of good health.

Bramble's quest eventually leads him north to Edinburgh, a city that Smollett himself visited briefly on at least two occasions and where, in the summer of 1766 while lodging with his widowed sister – 'a clever, spirited woman . . . possessed of a great deal of racy Scotch [sic] humour', according to one biographer[6] – at her flat in St John Street, he would have found himself well placed to absorb impressions of the city for use in *Humphry Clinker*.

Matthew Bramble's brief sojourn in Edinburgh provides Smollett with the ideal opportunity to impart his thoughts and observations on 'this hot-bed of genius' to his readers. 'The city', he wrote to his friend Dr Lewis on arrival, 'stands upon two hills, and the bottom between them; and, with all its defects, may well pass for the capital of a moderate kingdom.' One of those defects was undoubtedly that same 'evening effluvia' which was so sorely to trouble Boswell and Johnson a few years later. 'You are no stranger to [the inhabitants'] method of discharging all their impurities from their windows at a certain time of the night . . . a practice to which I can by no means be reconciled; for notwithstanding all the care that is taken by the scavengers to remove this nuisance every morning by break of day, enough still remains to offend the eyes, as well as other organs of those whom use had not hardened against all delicacy of sensation.' Apart from that, Bramble's company enjoyed ' . . . all the diversions of London . . . in a small compass'.[7]

Jeremy Melford positively hurled himself into the spirit of the place, but even he found one of the favourite local culinary dishes hard to digest. 'If I stay much longer at Edinburgh', he enthused at the end of a fortnight, 'I shall be changed into a downright Caledonian . . . but I am not yet Scotchman enough to relish their singed sheep's-head and haggis, which were provided one day . . . where we dined. The first put me in mind of the history of the Congo, in which I had read of negroes' heads sold publicly in the market; the last being a mess of minced lights, liver, suet, oatmeal, onions, and pepper, enclosed in a sheep's stomach, had a very sudden effect upon mine, and the delicate Mrs. Tabby changed colour . . .'[8]

Bramble, who planned to travel further north into the heart of Scotland, sounded a wistful note when, after a few weeks, the time came to quit the city. 'I protest, I shall leave with much regret. I am so far from thinking it any hardship to live in this country, that, if I was obliged to lead a town life, Edinburgh would certainly be [my] headquarters . . .'[9]

The Nineteenth Century

William and Dorothy Wordsworth arrived in Edinburgh on the evening of 15 September 1803, towards the end of a long touring holiday which had embraced the Trossachs, Glen Coe and Loch Lomond. They had set out from their home at Rydal in the Lake District almost exactly a month earlier, travelling as a party of three with their friend and fellow poet, Samuel Taylor Coleridge, who lived at nearby Keswick.

Coleridge and the Wordsworths had first met almost a decade earlier when, all in their mid-twenties, they had been West Country neighbours living in the shadow of the Quantock Hills. The two men had stepped out together on many a walking-tour over the intervening years and, each delighting in the admiration of the other, had been inspired by their friendship to ever greater heights of poetic achievement – including their collaboration on *Lyrical Ballads* published in 1798 – while William's sister Dorothy doted on both of them and made copious notes about their activities in her detailed journals.

However, by the time the trio left the Lake District in mid-August, bound for a six weeks' tour of the Scottish Highlands in their hired Irish jaunting car, chinks had begun to appear in their friendship, a state of affairs which did not bode well for the long holiday ahead. Poor weather soon took its toll on the travellers' spirits as they meandered northwards, and their primitive mode of transport only served to make matters worse. The jaunting car gave no protection against the elements, so that when it rained

– and it seems to have poured down almost incessantly during the early days of their trip – the vehicle's occupants were quickly soaked through. William and Dorothy withstood the inclement weather well, but Coleridge's spirits flagged. The party eventually broke up by mutual consent at Arrochar, with Coleridge deciding to press on alone and on foot while the Wordsworths persevered with their jaunting car.

William and Dorothy trundled into Edinburgh during the final week of their holiday and immediately put up at the White Hart in the Grassmarket, 'an inn which had been mentioned to us, and which we conjectured would better suit us than one in a more fashionable part of town,' explained Dorothy. 'It was not noisy and tolerably cheap.'[10] (This eighteenth-century coaching inn can still be seen today.) The daylight had almost gone by the time they arrived, so all thoughts of sightseeing were postponed until the following morning, but when dawn broke the weather proved a disappointment. It was 'downright dismal', complained Dorothy, 'and promising nothing but a wet day'. However, like all dogged tourists with only a short time at their disposal, the Wordsworths pressed on regardless. Bravely, they climbed to the exposed summit of Arthur's Seat from where, recorded Dorothy, 'we listened to the noises [below], which were blended in one loud indistinct buzz . . . a cloud of black smoke overhung the city, which combined with the rain and the mist to conceal the shapes of the houses – an obscurity which added much to the grandeur of the sound that proceeded from it. It was impossible to think of anything that was little or mean, the goings-on of trade, the strife of men, or everyday city business: the impression was one, and it was visionary; like the conceptions of our childhood of Bagdad or Balsora, when we have been reading the Arabian Nights Entertainments.'[11]

As Dorothy had predicted, the rain continued unabated throughout the day, but the Wordsworths refused to let it dampen their spirits, and were eager to fit in as much sightseeing as possible before leaving Edinburgh that same evening in order to call on Walter Scott at Lasswade. 'We walked industriously through the streets, street after street, and, in spite of wet and dirt, were exceedingly delighted. The Old Town, with its irregular houses, stage above stage, seen as we saw it, in the obscurity of a rainy day, hardly resembles the work of man, it is more like a piling up of rocks . . . I cannot attempt to describe what we saw so imperfectly, but must say that, high as my expectations had been raised, the city of Edinburgh surpassed all expectation.'[12]

A hastily arranged marriage drew the Romantic poet Percy Bysshe Shelley to Edinburgh briefly in the early nineteenth century. In August 1811, soon after being sent down from Oxford (where he had ruffled the feathers of the university authorities by writing and circulating a pamphlet on atheism), he travelled north accompanied by his bride-to-be, Harriet Westbrook, with whom he had eloped. The pair were extremely young – Shelley, the son of a Sussex MP, was nineteen, and Harriet only sixteen – when they were married at a clergyman's house in the Canongate. They spent just over a month honeymooning in Edinburgh, renting rooms in George Street. It was an inauspicious start to their married life, because the couple had very little money to support themselves at first. 'When Shelley reached Edinburgh his scanty resources were exhausted,' reported Edward Dowden in his *Life of Percy Bysshe Shelley* (1886). '[But] he . . . was fortunate in alighting on a good-humoured landlord, to whom he explained his position – his present need, his expectation of speedy relief [in the form of a quarterly allowance from his father], and the object of his journey to Scotland. Would he take them in, Shelley asked, advance them money to get married, and supply their wants until a remittance came? The landlord cheerily assented on one condition – that Shelley should treat himself . . . to a supper in honour of the wedding.'[13]

Sadly, after all, financial help was not forthcoming from Shelley's father, who heartily disapproved of his son's marriage and stopped his allowance, but the young poet was eventually bailed out by a generous uncle, thereafter allowing the newlyweds to live reasonably well. Even so, as Dowden explained, 'the most romantic of northern cities could lay no spell on [Shelley's] spirit. To the brilliant literary society of the Scottish capital he had no introduction; his eye was not fascinated by the presence of mountains and the sea; by the fantastic outlines of aerial piles seen amid the wreathing smoke of Auld Reekie . . . nor was his imagination kindled by storied house and palace, and the voices of old, forgotten far-off things which haunt their walls.'[14]

Two years later, during the autumn of 1813, the Shelleys were once again briefly in Edinburgh, lodging on this occasion in Frederick Street. Dowden suggests that the visit was prompted by the poet's need to evade creditors at home. Whatever the reason, Shelley's original plan had been to remain in Edinburgh for the winter but, by the end of November, he had left the city to go south, prompting one critic to describe the visit as 'one of Shelley's motiveless and costly freaks'.[15]

George Borrow was a Norfolk man, born at Dumpling Green in 1803. He died not far away at Oulton Broad in the neighbouring county of Suffolk seventy-eight years later but, in the meantime, he had spent much of his life wandering the highways and byways of Britain. He also ventured abroad. The itinerant nature of his existence is reflected in his autobiographical novels *Lavengro* (1851) and its sequel *The Romany Rye* (1857), books that were described by the early twentieth-century poet Edward Thomas as 'refined by dream and modified by romance'. Accounts of Borrow's travels can also be found in *The Bible in Spain* (1841) and *Wild Wales* (1862).

Borrow's father was a captain in the West Norfolk Militia, serving as a recruiting officer at the time of the Napoleonic Wars. In 1813, when Borrow was ten, the regiment was posted north to be billeted at Edinburgh Castle, 'into which [the men] marched with drums beating, colours flying, and a large train of baggage-waggons behind',[16] he recalled in *Lavengro*. Borrow was an adventurous and adaptable boy who, uprooted from his native rural East Anglia and transplanted to a large city in a foreign land, soon settled in to his fresh surroundings and forged new friendships. A boy called Davy Haggart, 'whom . . . I had seen enlisted on Leith Links to serve King George with drum and drumstick', was his special companion. (Sadly, Davy came to a sticky end when, in 1821, he was hanged for murder.) Borrow was educated at Edinburgh High School, despite his father's initial reservations. ''Tis said to be the best school in the whole island; but the idea of one's children speaking Scotch – broad Scotch! I must think the matter over.'[17]

The rock on which Borrow's new home stood fascinated the boy, 'a great crag which at first sight would seem to bid defiance to any feet save those of goats and chamois . . .' However, it was not long before Borrow was joining his young Edinburgh friends and scaling it regularly like a native of the place. 'I soon found that the rock contained all manner of strange crypts, crannies, and recesses, where owls nested, and the weasel brought forth her young,' he wrote. 'Here and there were small natural platforms, overgrown with long grass and various kinds of plants, where the climber, if so disposed, could stretch himself, and either give his eyes to sleep or his mind to thought; for capital places were these same platforms either for repose or meditation.'[18]

The West Norfolk Militia were stationed at Edinburgh Castle for almost two years, before returning to England at the end of the Napoleonic Wars. By this time, Captain Borrow's worst fears had been realised, when his son proclaimed that he had become 'a Scot in most things, particularly in language'.[19]

William Cobbett was born at Farnham, Surrey, in 1763 and died a mere four miles away at Ash in 1835. In an age when most people rarely ventured far from their native village, perhaps he could be regarded as very much a man of his time, but that would belie the true course of his life. During the seventy-two years which separated his birth and death, he served in the British Army in Canada and lived in the United States; he was a prisoner at Newgate and a farmer in Hampshire and Surrey. Finally, at the tail-end of his life, he was elected Member of Parliament for Oldham in Lancashire. However, Cobbett is probably best remembered today as the author of *Rural Rides* (1830), a book recounting his observations and experiences during journeys made on horseback through the eastern and southern counties of England in the 1820s, at a time when the country was undergoing its sometimes painful transition from an agricultural to an industrial society.

In the autumn of 1832, as an elderly man in his seventieth year and on the eve of his election to Parliament, Cobbett ventured north – travelling by stagecoach instead of on horseback as a slight concession to age – to cast his critical eye over the Lowlands of Scotland. He was not a man to disguise his thoughts, and his opinions could sometimes arouse strong passions in the breasts of others. After he had written uncharitably about Cheltenham, for example, following a visit he made in 1826, some of the inhabitants were moved to carry a burning effigy of him through the streets of the town. However, the denizens of Edinburgh – where Cobbett arrived in mid-October – had no excuse for such extreme behaviour. 'This is the finest city that I ever saw in my life', he declared after settling in, 'with its castle, its hills, its pretty little sea-port, conveniently detached from it, its vale of rich land lying all around, its lofty hills in the background, its views across the Firth . . . I think a great deal of the fine and well-ordered streets of shops . . . and I think still more of the absence of all that foppishness, and that affectation of carelessness, and that impudent assumption of superiority, that you see in almost all the young men that you meet with in the fashionable parts of the great towns of England. I was not disappointed; for I expected to find Edinburgh the finest city in the kingdom.'[20]

Mrs Elizabeth Gaskell was a literary contemporary of Thomas Carlyle, Charles Dickens and George Eliot, by all of whom she was much admired as a novelist. Born in London in 1810, she was brought up in the small Cheshire town of Knutsford, which she immortalised as 'Cranford'. The novel of that title, published in 1853, is a fine and minutely drawn portrait of provincial English life and manners, with much of the tale revolving around sweet Miss Matty, the rector's daughter, and her circle of genteel friends and neighbours. In contrast, much of her fiction – including *Mary Barton* (1848) and *North and South* (1855) – grew out of the environment she had known since her marriage, that of the gloomy manufacturing districts of early nineteenth-century Manchester, where she witnessed at first hand every day the appalling conditions endured by the poorest members of the industrial classes.

However, in Mrs Gaskell's 'Round the Sofa' (an Introduction to *My Lady Ludlow and Other Tales* (1859)), we are treated to a glimpse of mid-nineteenth-century Edinburgh. Her parents had moved to the city in 1801 after farming unsuccessfully in East Lothian, but they remained in Drummond Street for barely three years before travelling south to make their home in London.

Mrs Gaskell visited Edinburgh at least twice, the last occasion being in 1864 (the year before her death), when she travelled north to stay for a few weeks with a friend who was Professor of Natural History at the university. But her first sight of Edinburgh had probably been as a young woman in 1831, when she visited the city with a distant relation, Anne

Turner. Perhaps the pair were invited to attend one or two of the drawing-room soirées that graced Edinburgh's social life in those days, such as the one held at the home of the fictional Mrs Dawson and described by Miss Greatorex in 'Round the Sofa': 'We entered . . . the large square drawing-room . . . By-and-by Mrs. Dawson's maid brought in tea and macaroons for us . . . Then the door opened. We had come very early, and in came Edinburgh professors, Edinburgh beauties, and celebrities, all on their way to some other gayer and later party, but coming first to see Mrs. Dawson, and tell her their bon-mots, or their interests, or their plans . . . It was very brilliant and very dazzling, and gave enough to think about and wonder about for many days.'[21]

Mrs Gaskell also wrote one of the nineteenth century's most celebrated – and controversial – literary biographies, *The Life of Charlotte Brontë*, published in 1857. The author of *Jane Eyre* (1847) shared her remote parsonage home in the moorland village of Haworth, near Keighley, with her two sisters: Emily, the creator of *Wuthering Heights* (1847) and Anne, who wrote *The Tenant of Wildfell Hall* (1848), while their self-destructive brother Branwell hovered over them all. Unlike his sisters, he failed to make a great literary name for himself, although as a young man of eighteen he petitioned the editor of *Blackwood's Magazine* in Edinburgh on more than one occasion to consider his work. 'My resolution is to devote my ability to you . . .', he gushed in 1836. 'You have lost an able writer in James Hogg [who had died the previous year], and God grant you may gain one in [me].'[22]

Charlotte Brontë was not a great traveller, although she did visit Brussels in the early 1840s (where her experiences were reflected in two novels, *Villette* (1853) and *The Professor* (1857)), and she also went south to London a few years later. At the beginning of July 1850, she paid the briefest of visits to Edinburgh in the company of her publisher George Smith and his sister, after which she claimed that the two days she had passed sightseeing in 'mine own romantic town' '[were] as happy almost as any I ever spent . . . Who indeed that has once seen Edinburgh,' she wrote in a letter on 20 July, 'with its couchant crag-lion, but must see it again in dreams waking or sleeping?'[23] The reference to 'mine own romantic town' is drawn from Scott's poem, *Marmion*:

> Such dusky grandeur clothed the height
> Where the huge castle holds its state
> And all the steep slope down,
> Whose ridgy back heaves to the sky,
> Piled deep and massy, close and high,
> Mine own romantic town!

A few months later, Charlotte Brontë's impressions on reaching the summit of Arthur's Seat were still vivid in her memory. 'I shall not soon forget how I felt when . . . we all sat down and looked over the city, towards the sea and Leith.'[24]

Two major periodicals held particular sway in nineteenth-century Edinburgh. The *Edinburgh Review*, co-founded in 1802 by the Scottish judge and Member of Parliament, Lord Francis Jeffrey, 'elevated the public and literary position of Edinburgh to an extent which no one not living intelligently then can be made to comprehend', claimed Henry Cockburn. Jeffrey served as editor of the *Review* until 1829, and Sir Walter Scott, Thomas Carlyle and William Hazlitt were among the many famous literary contributors to its pages at various times. One of the periodical's distinguishing features was the excellent rates of pay offered by its publisher, Archibald Constable. His 'unheard-of prices', enthused Cockburn, 'drew authors from dens where they would otherwise have starved, and made Edinburgh a literary mart, famous with strangers, and the pride of its own citizens'.[25] The *Edinburgh Review* eventually ceased publication in 1929.

Blackwood's Magazine (originally called *The Edinburgh Monthly Magazine*), was founded in 1817 by another of the city's leading publishers, William Blackwood, and, like the *Edinburgh Review*, devoted some of its pages to literature. Unlike its closest rival, however, *Blackwood's* also serialised new fiction and John Blackwood, a son of the founder, was quick to snap up the three stories – 'The Sad Fortunes of the Rev. Amos Barton', 'Mr. Gilfil's Love Story' and 'Janet's Repentance' – which comprised George Eliot's first major work, *Scenes of Clerical Life*, issued as a volume in 1858 when she was in her late thirties.

George Eliot (the pseudonym used by Marian Evans to disguise the fact that she was a woman) became one of the most influential novelists of the nineteenth century. She scandalised straight-laced Victorian society by openly living unmarried with the journalist and critic George Lewes. With the exception of *Romola* (which appeared in the London-based *Cornhill Magazine*), all of George Eliot's major novels – including *Adam Bede* (1859), *The Mill on the Floss* (1860), *Middlemarch* (1871–2) and *Daniel Deronda* (1876) – made their first appearance as serials in the pages of *Blackwood's*. As a result, George Eliot was always grateful to John Blackwood for his encouragement over the course of many years.

Blackwood's Magazine outlived the *Edinburgh Review* by half a century, with its final issue appearing in 1980.

The Twentieth Century

The twentieth century was barely two years old when a young girl of nine or ten, called Cecily (Cissie) Fairfield, arrived in Edinburgh after moving north from London accompanied by her mother and sisters. By this time her father was permanently absent from home, and her mother had decided to return to Edinburgh because it was where she had been born and the place where she grew up. While still a young woman, Cissie adopted the name by which she later became famous and, as Rebecca West, she enjoyed a long and distinguished literary life which spanned much of the twentieth century (she died in 1983), making her mark as a journalist, critic and novelist.

The young girl was sent to school at George Watson's Ladies' College in George Square, just a short step away from her first Edinburgh home in Hope Park Square where, as she was to describe in her early novel, *The Judge* (1922), 'on three sides . . . small squat houses sat closely with a quarrelling air . . .'[26] After some time the Fairfields moved to Buccleuch Place, which was even closer to George Square. 'Mrs. Fairfield, brought up in Edinburgh, knew its tribal customs,' explains Victoria Glendinning in her biography, *Rebecca West: A Life* (1987). 'To Cissie, the Edinburgh set-up seemed "deplorable" . . . The Scottish relations seemed a depressing lot. In comparison with absent Papa and the Fairfield uncles, they were not "educated" people with contacts in the wider world – though their unmitigated Scottishness, Cissie liked to believe, had been enlivened in the eighteenth century by African blood from a Berber bride brought back by a soldier ancestor . . .'[27]

Cissie remained in Edinburgh for eight years, but she seems never really to have felt at home there. As time wore on she developed a passion for the theatre and, in 1910, after gaining a place at the Academy of Dramatic Art (as it was then called), she moved back to London, gladly leaving Edinburgh behind her for ever.

Rebecca West's first – and highly acclaimed – novel *The Return of the Soldier* was published in 1918. (It was made into a film as recently as 1982.) However, four years were to elapse before the appearance of her second book, *The Judge*, which is partly set against the background of the Edinburgh she had been familiar with as a child. Like the author of the novel, who had joined Edinburgh's Votes for Women club in her early teens, the heroine of the story, seventeen-year-old Ellen Melville, is a suffragette who sold the movement's newspaper

Votes for Women in Princes Street on Saturday afternoons. She is employed as a typist in the office of an Edinburgh lawyer, where 'she spent much of her time composing speeches which she knew she would always be too shy to deliver . . .'[28]

Ellen seems to have possessed a grudging affection for Edinburgh that appears to have been entirely lacking in Rebecca West's own life, but our fictional heroine shared with Stevenson a palpable dislike of its harsh climate. Gazing down from her office window on the home-going crowds of city workers, she watched 'as they came to the corner and met the full force of the east wind, and then pulled themselves upright and butted at it afresh with dour faces . . . Such inclemencies . . . she reckoned as the price one had to pay for the dignity of living in Edinburgh; which indeed gave it its dignity, since to survive anything so horrible proved one good rough stuff to govern the rest of the world . . .'[29]

John Buchan was a prolific author; a novelist, biographer and historian who, by the time of his death at the age of sixty-four, had published more than seventy books. Nowadays he is perhaps best remembered as the author of *The Thirty-Nine Steps* (the first of several counter-espionage thrillers that feature Richard Hannay as their hero), which appeared in 1915 and was memorably filmed by Alfred Hitchcock twenty years later. But in addition to numerous novels with contemporary and historical themes, such as *Huntingtower* (1922) and *Witch Wood* (1927), Buchan also published biographies of *Sir Walter Raleigh* (1911), *Sir Walter Scott* (1932) and *Oliver Cromwell* (1934), together with historical accounts of the First World War (1921–2) and the massacre at Glencoe (1933), and much more besides.

Born in Perth in 1875, and educated at Glasgow University and Brasenose College, Oxford, Buchan was called to the Bar in 1901. A few years later, following his marriage in 1907, he changed the direction his career was taking and became a partner in the old-established Edinburgh publishing firm of Thomas Nelson & Son. Although he was based predominantly at their London office, it was a move that caused him to make frequent visits to Nelson's Parkside works in the shadow of Salisbury Crags.

Buchan became editor of Nelson's short-lived magazine, the *Scottish Review*, a periodical that he perhaps over-optimistically envisaged becoming 'the centre of a Scottish school of letters, such as Edinburgh had a hundred years ago'.[30] However, when the magazine closed after just two years in operation owing to low circulation figures, Buchan turned his attention to editing the firm's famous Nelson Sixpenny Classics series of reprints together with other cheap editions of a broad range of literature.

During the first visit they made together to Edinburgh after their marriage, the Buchans stayed in a house which belonged to the Nelson family situated close to the Parkside works. 'It was enormous, even judged by the standards of yesterday,' recalled Buchan's wife, Susan, many years later, 'but we existed happily in a corner of it with two excellent Scots servants. The garden had sweeping green lawns and a view of Arthur's Seat which redeemed the gloom of the heavy carved woodwork and the sombre curtains . . .'[31]

When visiting the city on subsequent occasions, the couple stayed with their friends the Maitlands at 6 Heriot Row. 'Those who only know the Edinburgh of today,' lamented Lady Tweedsmuir in 1947 (Buchan had been raised to the peerage in 1935), 'with the weary pattern of queues for overfull trams or for inferior meals, cannot realise the charm it had many years ago. In August and September her squares were empty of life. The large houses looked blank and shut up and grass grew between the cobbles in the streets, while the feet of the passer-by echoed in the silence . . . There were odd little shops in the back streets which sold such unusual objects as large sea-shells and others where you could buy sugar mice with cotton tails . . .'[32]

Buchan eventually resigned from Nelson's in 1929, by which time he was sitting as Member of Parliament for the Scottish Universities. For most writers, to produce an output as large and varied as Buchan's would in itself have been a full-time occupation, but his was a life that was also devoted to public service. In 1933, and again the following year, the King appointed him High Commissioner to the General Assembly of the Church of Scotland. 'The King's Commissioner opens and closes the Assembly, appears daily at its meetings, and fulfils a multitude of other engagements,' explained Buchan in his posthumously published autobiography, *Memory Hold-the-Door* (1940). 'For a fortnight he lives in the Palace of Holyroodhouse, where he entertains the Church and the World according to his means and his inclination . . . Holyroodhouse used to be the last word in shabby discomfort; the High Commissioner had to bring his own plate, linen and other accessories, and bivouac in windy chambers where the rats scampered. Now it is like a well-appointed country house, and I think the west drawing-room, which looks out on Arthur's Seat, one of the pleasantest rooms I have ever entered.'[33]

In 1937, Buchan (now Lord Tweedsmuir) was elected Chancellor of Edinburgh University, by which time he had been absent from Britain for two years while serving as Governor-General of Canada. He paid a brief visit to the city in July to attend his installation before returning to Ottawa a few months later. After his death in February 1940, his ashes were brought back to England and buried in the churchyard at Elsfield, the Oxfordshire village which had been his home since 1919.

Sir Compton Mackenzie is probably most closely associated today with that most durable of comic novels, *Whisky Galore*, which was first published in 1947. He was the prolific author of more than ninety books – other highly successful novels included *Carnival* (1912) and *Sinister Street* (1913–14) – but he also wrote plays, biographies, and volumes of poetry and criticism. However, his fictional account of the occasion, during the Second World War, when the contents of a wrecked ship laden with whisky were washed up on the shores of the tiny Hebridean island of Eriskay, became one of his greatest popular successes. (When the novel was filmed in 1948, as one of the now legendary Ealing comedies, Mackenzie played the role of Captain Mackechnie.)

Born in Hartlepool in 1883, Mackenzie made his home in various parts of the country – London, the Cotswold town of Burford, Beech in Hampshire, the Channel Islands and the Outer Hebrides – before finally settling in Edinburgh in 1953. The house in which he chose to spend the twilight years of his life was 31 Drummond Place, an elegant residence in the city's New Town, although Mackenzie had harboured some reservations about the move before making his final decision. 'At this date', he wrote, 'it was touch and go whether Drummond Place would maintain the dignity it had enjoyed until the Second World War had over "popularised" it. The railings of the big central garden had been pulled down in that fatuous campaign for scrap iron, and the residents were just getting together to re-fence the garden and prevent it becoming the playground of destructive youngsters.'[34]

Mackenzie's fellow novelist, Eric Linklater, explains how it was old age that finally persuaded the author of *Whisky Galore* to take up permanent residence in Edinburgh (although he almost invariably spent each winter abroad): '[Mackenzie said] he got the most of his entertainment from conversation, and Edinburgh was the home of good talk. He is himself among the best of talkers, but a generous listener.'[35]

It was at Drummond Place, surrounded by his vast collection of books, and often writing and receiving visitors while lying in bed until well into the afternoon, that Mackenzie set to work on his monumental ten-volume autobiography, *My Life and Times*, which appeared at intervals between 1963 and 1971.

Among those events relating to his years at Drummond Place, Mackenzie recalled the time in 1958 when he attended the installation of his friend, the actor James Robertson Justice, as Rector of Edinburgh University. The ceremony was presided over by the Duke of Edinburgh, acting in his capacity as the University's Chancellor and, once the formalities were completed, all three men retired to Drummond Place for some welcome refreshment. 'It was imperative to conceal the Duke's visit from reporters and cameramen for his own relaxation,' Mackenzie recalled. 'We were successful in keeping the secret and while [they] were chasing one clue after another all over Edinburgh, the Duke himself . . . and the new Rector of the University were enjoying an old malt whisky . . . uncorked for the occasion.'[36]

In addition to being a busy author – among the novels he wrote while living at Drummond Place was *Rockets Galore* (1957), which took the reader back to the fictional Hebridean islands Little and Great Todday of *Whisky Galore* fame – Mackenzie also developed into a much sought-after radio broadcaster and he appeared frequently on television as well. He also acquired a probably well-deserved reputation for eccentricity, at one time permitting his future sister-in-law (who later, somewhat confusingly, became his third wife) to open a hairdressing salon in the basement of 31 Drummond Place. The decision, which may well have raised a few eyebrows among Mackenzie's closest friends, prompted Linklater to wonder at the time whether '31 Drummond Place will become as famous, and be as long remembered, as Ramsay the perruquier's shop in the Luckenbooths'.[37] (Allan Ramsay, it will be recalled, had been a wig-maker before establishing himself as an eighteenth-century poet.)

Mackenzie spent the last nineteen years of his life at Drummond Place, where he died in November 1972 not far short of his ninetieth birthday and by which time, according to the diplomat and author Robert Bruce Lockhart, he had long been regarded 'with the Castle, the Royal Mile, Holyrood, Rosslyn Chapel and the Forth Bridge [as] one of the sights of Edinburgh'.[38]

'Edinburgh', wrote Muriel Spark, 'is the place that I, a constitutional exile, am essentially exiled from . . . It is a place where I could not hope to be understood . . . Nevertheless, it is the place where I was first understood. James Gillespie's Girls' School, set in solid state among the green meadows, showed an energetic faith in my literary life.'[39] As time would prove, that faith was well placed, and since those days during the 1920s and 1930s Muriel Spark has become one of Britain's foremost writers. She published her first – highly successful – novel, *The Comforters*, in 1957 at the perhaps relatively late age of thirty-nine, and subsequently established her reputation with many others, including *Memento Mori* (1959), *The Ballad of Peckham Rye* (1960), and the novel which remains possibly her most famous work, *The Prime of Miss Jean Brodie* (1961). Set in Edinburgh during the 1930s, the book has been filmed, played on the stage, made into a television series and read by millions of people throughout the world.

Muriel Spark was born in 1918 at Bruntsfield Place, and grew up there close to the Meadows. For twelve years she was a pupil at James Gillespie's where, as she explained in her autobiography *Curriculum Vitae* (1992), she 'fell into Miss Kay's hands at the age of eleven. It might well be said that she fell into my hands. Little did she know, little did I know, that she bore within her the seeds of the future Miss Jean Brodie . . . She entered my imagination immediately. I started to write about her even then.'[40]

The Prime of Miss Jean Brodie recounts the story of the eponymous Edinburgh schoolmistress and, in particular, the influence she exerts over her select group of sixteen-year-old pupils (famously described as her 'crème de la crème'), set in the city's fictional Marcia Blaines School for Girls. Miss Brodie, 'in many ways . . . an Edinburgh spinster of the deepest dye . . .', whose girls were 'vastly informed on a lot of subjects irrelevant to the authorized curriculum . . .', instilled in her set the maxim that 'Goodness, Truth and Beauty come first'. In later life one of Miss Brodie's pupils, Eunice Gardiner, describes her former teacher as 'full of culture. She was an Edinburgh Festival all on her own.'[41]

Muriel Spark left Edinburgh when she was still a young woman and, despite paying visits over the years, has lived much of her life elsewhere. However, in writing *The Prime of Miss Jean Brodie*, she has given to the world what is probably the most widely known novel with an Edinburgh setting to emerge since the Second World War.

'Golden Ages' are notoriously elusive; they creep up on us unawares, then melt into the past even before we know they have arrived. They can only truly claim their status when posterity has served to put the years at a safe distance and these palmy days are measured against what preceded and followed them. Thus we view Scott's long reign in Edinburgh – and to some extent that of Stevenson also – as the city's finest literary hour, and perhaps we are justified in doing so. However, it would be interesting to discover how an observer engaged on a book of this kind in one hundred or so years' time might assess the literary climate of Edinburgh at the close of the twentieth century.

Pre-eminent among Edinburgh's native poets in recent times stands Norman MacCaig, who died in 1996 after spending nearly forty years of his working life as a schoolteacher and headmaster in the city. He was also appointed a creative writing fellow at Edinburgh University, where he had once been an undergraduate. MacCaig was a prolific poet whose work was heavily influenced both by the city of his birth and by the wilder landscapes of the Highlands and the Outer Hebrides (his mother was a native of Harris). He published many volumes of poems during his lifetime (beginning with *Far Cry* in 1943), and his *Collected Poems* appeared in 1985, the year before he was awarded the coveted Queen's Gold Medal for Poetry. He wrote extensively about Edinburgh, of course, producing many vivid and atmospheric vignettes of the city, such as the evocative 'Edinburgh Courtyard in July':

> Hot light is smeared as thick as paint
> On these ramshackle tenements. Stones smell
> of dust. Their hoisting into quaint
> Crowsteps, corbels, covered with fool and saint,
> Hold fathoms of heat, like water in a well . . .[42]

In 'Milne's Bar', MacCaig captures the atmosphere in one of Edinburgh's 'literary' pubs which, like its Fitzrovian counterparts in London during the years immediately following the Second World War, served as a meeting-place for poets and writers, and where

> Cigarette smoke floated
> in an eastern way
> a yard above the slopped tables . . .[43]

There has been an abundance of novels published during the 1990s alone that employ Edinburgh as a setting to a greater or lesser extent (Lownie's *Literary Companion to Edinburgh* lists more than eighty such titles). These include the series of popular crime novels – beginning with *Knots & Crosses* in 1987 – written by Fife-born Ian Rankin and which feature Detective Inspector John Rebus as their central character. Rebus, whose various cases have taken the reader on a journey to all corners of Edinburgh, has now become sufficiently celebrated to be mentioned in the same breath as Colin Dexter's Morse and Ruth Rendell's Wexford.

Joan Lingard was born in Edinburgh during the early 1930s and, after growing up in Belfast, has returned to spend most of her adult and working life in her native city. She has written extensively, and with great success, for children and adults alike over a long and distinguished literary career. Her innovative series of novels for young people, beginning with *The Twelfth of July* and inspired by the troubles in Northern Ireland, have remained popular ever since their first appearance in the 1970s. She draws on Edinburgh as a setting in several of her novels for adults, including – in more recent years – *Reasonable Doubts* (1986) and *After Colette* (1993). Her book, *The Kiss* (2002), mirrors the painter Gwen John's passion for the sculptor Auguste Rodin through a fifteen-year-old female pupil's infatuation with her art teacher. Rooted in the Colonies, 'a small enclave of Victorian artisans' houses . . . which lie alongside the Water of Leith . . .',[44] where the beleaguered art teacher and his family live, the tale visits a modern-day Edinburgh 'bristling with new coffee houses offering cappuccino and caffé latte and croissants plain, almond or au chocolat', while the homeless still plead for alms close by at the foot of the Playfair Steps and along Princes Street, where they 'are to be seen dotted at regular intervals . . . with their dogs and pieces of cardboard saying HOMELESS AND HUNGRY . . .'[45]

The underbelly of modern-day Edinburgh is captured unflinchingly in *Trainspotting* (1993) by Irvine Welsh. One of the great popular novels of the 1990s, it is also one of those landmark works of fiction that defines a place, a time and a generation.

Trainspotting gives the reader a graphic and uncompromising picture of a less affluent and drug-fuelled Edinburgh through the exploits of a group of young people who, as one contemporary review memorably phrased it, 'ride the down escalator of opportunity in the nation's capital'. A decade on, and devotees of Renton, Sick Boy, Begbie and Spud have been able to re-acquaint themselves with this hapless quartet, and an Edinburgh portrayed by Irvine Welsh, in *Porno* (2002).

Postscript

EDINBURGH EN FÊTE

For over half a century, Edinburgh during the month of August has played host to its world-renowned International Festival. This is a time when vacant hotel rooms and empty car parking spaces are almost impossible to find; weeks when the city is filled to capacity with traffic and visitors and, no matter where you turn, it seems that you are never more than a stone's throw from some form of artistic endeavour.

The Festival was established during those bleak and austerity-ridden days of 1947, when a celebration of international music and drama seemed to offer the best avenue of hope for the future after more than five years of conflict on the European and world stage. Obviously, a great deal of thought was given to finding a suitable location for an event of such significance, the founding fathers believing that the city eventually selected 'should, like Salzburg, have considerable scenic and picturesque appeal and . . . be set in a country likely to be attractive to tourists and foreign visitors'. Other essential requirements included 'a sufficient number of theatres, concert halls and open spaces for the adequate staging of a programme of an ambitious and varied character . . .'[1] Edinburgh fitted the bill to perfection.

From the outset, the Festival attracted some of the world's finest musicians and most prominent theatrical figures. Bruno Walter and the Vienna Philharmonic Orchestra, Tyrone Guthrie, John Gielgud and Richard Burton were all early participants. The breadth of the Festival swiftly increased so that, within a few years of its inauguration, visitors could also enjoy productions of ballet and opera, art exhibitions, a film festival and, of course, the pageantry of the Edinburgh Military Tattoo.

Around the great central pillar of the so-called 'official' Festival, the phenomenon memorably described by George Bruce in his book *Festival in the North* (1975) as 'the enormous unfenced field of the Fringe'[2] has grown ever larger, and can be found every year flourishing – or in some cases wilting – at venues across the city, ranging from the more prestigious Assembly Rooms and the Pleasance to seemingly almost any spare room, community centre, church hall, public garden or courtyard that can be pressed into service as a performance space or display area. Every conceivable art form is represented, and it is impossible to walk more than a hundred yards along any main street during the Festival period without a flyer being thrust into one's hand advertising the details of one event or another. Theatre productions on the Fringe are always staggeringly diverse (and, it must be said, of highly variable quality), ranging in 2002, for example, from the ceremony and ritual of a Japanese Nōh play to the internationally successful and highly diverting 'Puppetry of the Penis'.

While the organisers of the 'official' Festival programme have always shown a great willingness to diversify, there remained for some years an important aspect of the arts that was being to a great extent overlooked. In fact, it was not until the late 1960s that writers and literature in general came to be properly represented, when a number of 'Meet the Author' sessions were arranged. Initially, these events were largely based around Scottish writers, with Joan Lingard, Nigel Tranter and Lavinia Derwent among the first authors to appear. The poets Robert Garioch, Norman MacCaig and Hugh MacDiarmid (the pseudonym of C.M. Grieve) were also early contributors. Before long, however, writers such as Jane Gardam, Melvyn Bragg and Brigid Brophy were being drawn to Edinburgh from further afield, and 'Meet the Author' sessions were conducted each day at 11 a.m. throughout the run of the Festival, rather than for just one week of it, as had originally been the case.[3]

'Meet the Author' continued as a feature during the Festival throughout the 1970s and early 1980s, and its growing reputation in literary circles attracted an ever broader spectrum of writers. The sessions were held at various hotels around the city over the years, before finally coming to rest at the Roxburghe on Charlotte Square, a spot that was destined to be of particular significance in the future development of what would eventually become the Edinburgh International Book Festival.

A plan, supported by various leading publishers and other commercial sponsors, to link the promotion of books, reading and literature to the 1983 Edinburgh International Festival (although organised separately from it), was reported by *The Bookseller* at the end of 1982.[4] In a letter published a few weeks later, on 15 January 1983, the newly appointed Book Festival Director, Tony Gould Davies, explained the purpose of the event in more detail. 'The objective of the festival', he wrote, 'is to have a major consumer orientated book event, associated with the Edinburgh Festival, supported by relevant events and celebrities from all media, to increase the awareness of the range and depth of books available, and to sell as many books as possible.'[5] Opinions are divided, among those people who have been closely involved over the years, as to whether or not the founding of the Book Festival in its present form grew naturally out of the well-established 'Meet the Author' event held each year but, to the layman at least, it is difficult to view the transition as anything other than an entirely logical progression. Jenny Brown, who served as Director of the Book Festival from 1983 until 1991, points to John Calder's International Literary Conference held in 1962 as a major landmark in Edinburgh's literary history while believing that the 'Meet the Author' sessions had a more direct connection with the development of the Book Festival as we now know it.[6]

Charlotte Square Gardens was chosen as the site for what one contemporary press report heralded as a 'carnival of books', a literary extravaganza, lasting for two weeks, that was designed to attract adults and children alike and which, in 1983, cost around £120,000 to mount. (Today's budget is over £1 million.) Temporary buildings in the form of marquees were erected to accommodate the wide variety of events that had been planned, and which included talks, demonstrations, exhibitions, book-signings, a Children's Book Fair and, of course, 'Meet the Author' sessions. Around 30,000 visitors found their way into Charlotte Square Gardens during the course of the first Book Festival, with nearly 200 publishers participating by displaying and selling their books and with over 100 authors in attendance.

Although the 1983 Book Festival was originally intended to be a one-off event, its resounding commercial success led to the decision to establish it on a biennial basis (there was no question of mounting it annually at this stage), and the huddle of large tents in Charlotte Square Gardens seemed destined to become something of a landmark in Edinburgh's literary life. Subsequently, the Book Festival was held every two years until 1997 when it became an annual event at last.

The Book Festival has grown massively in size and stature over the past two decades, to become what is probably the world's leading event in its field. Every genre of writing is represented, from fiction, biography and poetry to cookery, politics and travel. There is always a lively programme of events for children as well, together with visits by many leading authors for young people. During her time as Director, Jenny Brown saw the scope of the event broaden considerably, with the early emphasis on Scottish writers and publishers giving way to an increasingly international dimension. 'We invited authors who had important things to say,' she explains, 'even if they did not have a new book to promote.' One of the Book Festival's great achievements over the years, she believes, is that it has become such an important platform for discussion.[7]

The continuing success of the Book Festival stems partly from its ready ability to evolve with the times, and its eagerness to embrace each new wave of promising literary talent and fresh or innovative forms of writing. Although the present-day Festival has been described as 'the biggest celebration of the written word in the world', it has not become impersonal for either participants or visitors, and many of those authors taking part attest to the warmth of the proceedings. Kate Atkinson, for example, whose first novel *Behind the Scenes at the Museum* was chosen as the Whitbread Book of the Year in 1995, thinks 'it is certainly the nicest book festival [she has] been to. Everyone is very friendly and makes you feel they are putting the author first.'[8] Writing in the newspaper *Scotland on Sunday*, author and politician Roy Hattersley believes that each of Britain's major book festivals – Cheltenham, Hay-on-Wye and Dartington – are 'a delight to attend [but] . . . the Edinburgh Book Festival has the incomparable advantage of being held in Edinburgh – still the most elegant city in the United Kingdom . . . At Edinburgh', he continues, 'speakers are guaranteed an audience which is as lively as it is friendly.'[9]

Judging by recent statistics, the Book Festival's long-term future seems assured. In 2010, 200,000 visitors – almost seven times the number achieved in 1983 – were drawn into the literary Mecca of Charlotte Square Gardens, and the programme featured 870 authors drawn from forty-nine different countries. Among those taking party were the Nobel Prize-winning poet

Seamus Heaney, the current Poet Laureate Carol Ann Duffy, the acclaimed American novelist Joyce Carol Oates and many other major literary figures, including A.S. Byatt, Philip Pullman, Ian Rankin, Roddy Doyle and Jeannette Winterson.[10]

The thriving programme of events held for children each year – well over 22,000 attended the Royal Bank of Scotland's Children's Programme in 2010[11] – no doubt encourages many young people to develop an early and enduring interest in books and reading. Perhaps it is not too fanciful to speculate that some of the youngest visitors to the Book Festival marquees during these early years of the twenty-first century may, as very elderly bookworms themselves and with great-grandchildren of their own, be present when (as surely must be the case) the Edinburgh International Book Festival receives its centenary telegram of congratulations from Buckingham Palace in 2083.

SOURCE NOTES

(Place of publication is London unless stated otherwise)

One: Boswell and Johnson

1. Daniel Defoe (ed. Pat Rogers), *A Tour through the Whole Island of Great Britain* (Webb & Bower/Michael Joseph, 1989), p. 205.
2. Edward Topham, *Letters from Edinburgh* (1774), (Lang Syne, Glasgow, 1989 edn), p. 7.
3. Oliphant Smeaton, *William Dunbar* (Oliphant Anderson and Ferrier, Edinburgh, 1898), pp. 65 and 71.
4. Quoted in James Boswell (ed. Christopher Hibbert), *The Life of Samuel Johnson* (Penguin, 1979 edn), p. 96.
5. James Boswell (ed. Hugh M. Milne), *Edinburgh Journals 1767–1786* (Mercat Press edn, Edinburgh, 2001), p. 173.
6. Quoted in Boswell, *The Life of Samuel Johnson*, p. 173.
7. James Boswell (ed. R.W. Chapman), *The Journal of a Tour to the Hebrides* (Oxford University Press, 1924 edn, reprinted 1979), p. 173.
8. Topham, *Letters*, p. 9.
9. Quoted in Christopher Hibbert, *The Personal History of Samuel Johnson* (Longman, 1971), pp. 131–2.
10. Boswell, *The Journal of a Tour to the Hebrides*, p. 174.
11. Ibid., p. 427.
12. Samuel Johnson (ed. R.W. Chapman), *A Journey to the Western Islands of Scotland* (Oxford University Press, 1924 edn, reprinted 1979), p. 3.
13. Quoted in Iain Finlayson, *The Moth and the Candle: A Life of James Boswell* (Constable, 1984), p. 241.
14. Eric Linklater, *Edinburgh* (Newnes, 1960), p. 119.

Two: Robert Burns

1. Quoted in Ian McIntyre, *Dirt & Deity: A Life of Robert Burns* (HarperCollins, 1995), p. 81.
2. Quoted in David Carroll, *Burns Country* (Sutton Publishing, Stroud, 1999), p. 20.
3. Quoted in Ibid., p. 20.
4. Quoted in Robert Chambers (ed.), *The Life and Works of Robert Burns* (4 vols), Vol. 2 (W & R Chambers, Edinburgh, 1856 edn), p. 4.
5. Ibid., p. 6.
6. Quoted in Ibid., p. 6.
7. Quoted in Ibid., p. 6.
8. Henry Cockburn, *Memorials of His Time* (A & C Black, Edinburgh, 1856), p. 169.
9. Robert Chambers, *Traditions of Edinburgh* (1824), (W & R Chambers, Edinburgh, 1967 edn), p. 104.
10. Smeaton, *Allan Ramsay* (Oliphant Anderson and Ferrier, Edinburgh, 1896), p. 57.
11. Chambers, *Traditions*, p. 15.
12. Ibid., p. 339.
13. Smeaton, *Allan Ramsay*, p. 116.
14. Chambers, *Traditions*, p. 14.
15. Quoted in Chambers, *The Life and Works of Robert Burns*, p. 51.
16. Quoted in McIntyre, *Dirt & Deity*, p. 120.
17. Quoted in Chambers, p. 55.
18. Ibid., p. 32.
19. Quoted in J.G. Lockhart, *The Life of Sir Walter Scott*, Vol. 1 (A & C Black, Edinburgh, 1888 edn), pp. 41–2.
20. Quoted in A.B. Grosart, *Robert Fergusson* (Oliphant Anderson and Ferrier, Edinburgh, 1898), pp. 10–11.
21. Grosart, p. 159.
22. Quoted in Ibid., p. 15.
23. Quoted in Ibid., p. 13.
24. Quoted in Chambers, p. 64.
25. Quoted in Ibid., p. 177.
26. Quoted in Ibid., p. 184.
27. Quoted in W.H. Davies (ed.), *Burns's Poetical Works* (Wm. Collins, n/d), p. 581.
28. Chambers, *Traditions*, pp. 358–9.
29. Chambers, *Life and Works of Robert Burns*, p. 257.
30. Michael Schmidt, *Lives of the Poets* (Weidenfeld & Nicolson, 1998), p. 345.

Three: Sir Walter Scott

1. Quoted in Rosemary Ashton, *George Eliot. A Life* (Hamish Hamilton, 1996), p. 313.
2. Cockburn, *Memorials of His Time*, pp. 211–12.
3. Quoted in Lockhart, *Life of Sir Walter Scott*, p. 3.
4. Quoted in Ibid., pp. 13–15.
5. Quoted in Ibid., p. 19.
6. Quoted in Ibid., pp. 25 and 32.
7. Ibid., p. 104.
8. Ibid., p. 150.
9. Ibid., p. 270.
10. Cockburn, *Memorials*, pp. 280–1.
11. Quoted in Rosaline Masson, *Edinburgh* (A & C Black, 1912), pp. 140–1.

12. Andrew Lang, *The Life and Letters of John Gibson Lockhart* (2 vols), (John C. Nimmo, 1897), p. 121.
13. Quoted in Ibid., p. 114.
14. Quoted in Ibid., p. 117.
15. Cockburn, *Memorials*, pp. 267–8.
16. See Masson, *Edinburgh*, pp. 138–9.
17. Quoted in Sir George Douglas, *James Hogg* (Oliphant Anderson and Ferrier, Edinburgh, 1899), p. 38.
18. Lockhart, *Life*, p. 124.
19. Ibid., p. 145.
20. Douglas, *James Hogg*, p. 53.
21. Quoted in Edith C. Batho, *The Ettrick Shepherd* (Cambridge University Press, 1927), pp. 107–8.
22. Sir Walter Scott, *The Abbot* (1820), (A & C Black, 1897 edn), Ch. 17, p. 158.
23. Scott, *The Heart of Midlothian* (1818), (A & C Black, 1897 edn), Ch. 7, pp. 77–8.
24. Lockhart, *Life*, p. 394.
25. Cockburn, *Memorials*, p. 430.
26. Ibid., p. 431.
27. W.E.K. Anderson (ed.), *The Journal of Sir Walter Scott* (Oxford University Press edn, 1972), pp. 67–8.
28. Ibid., pp. 89–90.
29. Ibid., p. 114.
30. Ibid., pp. 321, 392, 397, 429.
31. David Masson, *Edinburgh Sketches and Memories* (A & C Black, Edinburgh, 1892), p. 209.

Four: Thomas De Quincey
1. Edward Sackville-West, *A Flame in Sunlight* (Cassell & Co., 1936), p. 178.
2. Ibid., p. 227.
3. Sir Walter Scott, *Short Stories* (Oxford University Press, The World's Classics edn, 1934), p. 30.
4. Quoted in H.S. Salt, *De Quincey* (G. Bell & Sons, 1910), p. 31.
5. Quoted in Ibid., p. 31.
6. Quoted in Andrew Pennycook, *Literary and Artistic Landmarks of Edinburgh* (The Albyn Press, Edinburgh, 1973), p. 106.
7. Quoted in Salt, *De Quincey*, p. 33.
8. David Masson, Preface to *The Collected Writings of Thomas De Quincey* (14 vols), (A & C Black, Edinburgh, 1889).
9. Sackville-West, *Flame in Sunlight*, p. 292.
10. Masson, Preface.
11. Quoted in Hugh Sykes Davies, *Thomas De Quincey* (Longmans, Green & Co., 1964), p. 35.

Five: Thomas Carlyle
1. Thomas Carlyle (ed. Charles Eliot Norton), *Reminiscences* (2 vols), (Macmillan & Co., 1887 edn).
2. Ibid., Vol. 1, p. 222.
3. Ibid., p. 223.
4. Ibid., p. 223.
5. Quoted in David Masson, *Edinburgh Sketches and Memories*, pp. 274–5.

6. Carlyle, *Reminiscences*, Vol. 1, p. 104.
7. J.A. Froude, *Life of Carlyle* (4 vols, 1882 and 1884), (ed. John Clubbe), (John Murray, 1979), p. 140.
8. Quoted in Masson, *Edinburgh Sketches and Memories*, pp. 329 and 353.
9. Thea Holme, *The Carlyles at Home* (Oxford University Press, 1979 edn), p. 59.
10. Froude, *Life*, p. 204.
11. Carlyle, *Reminiscences*, Vol. 2, p. 79.
12. Froude, *Life*, p. 207.
13. Quoted in Ibid., p. 282.
14. Quoted in Ian Campbell, *Thomas Carlyle* (The Saltire Society edn, Edinburgh, 1993), p. 194.
15. Carlyle, *Reminiscences*, Vol. 2, p. 247.
16. Letter to the author from Professor Ian Campbell, dated 29 August 2002.

Six: Charles Dickens

1. Quoted in Edgar Johnson, *Charles Dickens: His Tragedy and Triumph* (Allen Lane, 1977 edn), p. 75.
2. Una Pope-Hennessy, *Charles Dickens* (Chatto & Windus, 1945), p. 32.
3. Charles Dickens, *The Pickwick Papers* (Penguin English Library, 1972 edn), pp. 778–9.
4. Quoted in David Paroissien, *Selected Letters of Charles Dickens* (Macmillan Press, 1985), p. 33.
5. Quoted in Johnson, *Charles Dickens*, p. 188.
6. Quoted in Pope-Hennessy, *Charles Dickens*, p. 128.
7. Quoted in W. Forbes Gray, 'The Edinburgh Relatives and Friends of Dickens', in *The Dickensian*, 1926 and 1927, p. 218.
8. Quoted in Peter Ackroyd, *Dickens* (Sinclair-Stevenson, 1990), p. 329.
9. Quoted in Forbes Gray, 'The Edinburgh Relatives', p. 19.
10. Ibid., p. 21.
11. Quoted in Ibid., p. 21.
12. Quoted in Ibid., p. 22.
13. Quoted in David Carroll, *A Literary Tour of Gloucestershire and Bristol* (Alan Sutton Publishing, Stroud, 1994), p. 142.
14. Quoted in Pope-Hennessy, *Charles Dickens*, p. 450.
15. Quoted in Trevor Royle, *Precipitous City: The Story of Literary Edinburgh*, (Mainstream Publishing, Edinburgh, 1980), p. 150.

Seven: Robert Louis Stevenson

1. J.M. Barrie, *An Edinburgh Eleven* (1889), (Hodder & Stoughton, 1924 edn), p. 111.
2. See Stevenson, *A Child's Garden of Verses* (1885), (Penguin Books/Puffin Story Books 1952 edn), p. 33.

3. Stevenson, 'A College Magazine' in *Memories and Portraits* (Chatto & Windus/ Cassell & Co./Wm. Heinemann/ Longmans Green & Co., Swanston edn, Vol. 9, 1911), p. 36.
4. Linklater, *Edinburgh*, p. 35.
5. Quoted in Jenni Calder, *RLS: A Life Study* (Hamish Hamilton, 1980), p. 16.
6. Stevenson, 'A Penny Plain and Twopence Coloured', in *Memories and Portraits*, p. 116.
7. Stevenson, 'The Manse', in *Memories and Portraits*, pp. 61–2.
8. Stevenson, *St. Ives* (1897), (Richard Drew Publishing edn, 1990), p. 48.
9. Stevenson, 'An Old Scots Gardener', in *Memories and Portraits*, p. 46.
10. Stevenson, 'Pastoral', in *Memories and Portraits*, p. 54.
11. Sidney Colvin (ed.), *The Letters of Robert Louis Stevenson Vol. 1 1868–1880* (Methuen & Co., 1911), p. 6.
12. Quoted in Hunter Davies, *The Teller of Tales: In Search of Robert Louis Stevenson* (Sinclair-Stevenson, 1994), p. 37.
13. Stevenson, 'Some College Memories', in *Memories and Portraits*, p. 20.
14. Colvin (ed.), *Letters*, p. 202.
15. Stevenson, *Edinburgh: Picturesque Notes* (1878), (Chatto & Windus, 1912 edn), p. 271.
16. Ibid., p. 296.
17. Ibid., p. 307.
18. Quoted in J.A. Hammerton, *Barrie: The Story of a Genius* (Sampson, Low, Marston & Co., 1929), p. 55.
19. Linklater, *Edinburgh*, p. 37.
20. Claire Harman's essay on Robert Louis Stevenson in Kate Marsh (ed.), *Writers and their Houses* (Hamish Hamilton, 1993), p. 422.

Eight: W.E. Henley
1. Colvin (ed.), *Letters*, p. 180.
2. Roden Shields, 'A Blurred Memory of Childhood', in *Cornhill Magazine*, August 1905, pp. 223, 226, 227, 228.
3. Colvin (ed.), *Letters*, p. 185.
4. Stevenson, 'Talk and Talkers', in *Memories and Portraits*, p. 88.
5. Kennedy Williamson, *W.E. Henley, A Memoir* (Harold Shaylor, 1930), p. 83.
6. Ibid., p. 189.

Nine: Sir Arthur Conan Doyle
1. Sir Arthur Conan Doyle, *Memories and Adventures* (Hodder & Stoughton, 1924), p. 7.
2. Ibid., p. 12.
3. Ibid., p. 10.
4. Ibid., p. 11.
5. Ibid., p. 15.
6. Ibid., p. 22.
7. Ibid., p. 34.
8. Ibid., p. 30.
9. Doyle, *The Firm of Girdlestone* (Chatto & Windus, 1890), Ch. 5.

10. Ibid.
11. Doyle, 'His First Operation', in *Round the Red Lamp* (Smith, Elder & Co., 1903), pp. 15–16.
12. Doyle, *Memories and Adventures*, p. 25.
13. Doyle, *A Study in Scarlet* (1887), (Ulverscroft edn, Leicester, N/D), pp. 14, 26
14. Doyle, *Memories and Adventures*, p. 26.
15. Ibid., p. 202.

Ten: J.M. Barrie

1. Barrie, *Margaret Ogilvy* (1896), (Hodder & Stoughton, 1925 edn), pp. 4–5.
2. Ibid., p. 39.
3. Doyle, *Memories and Adventures*, p. 23.
4. Quoted in Hammerton, *Barrie: The Story of a Genius*, p. 70.
5. Ibid., p. 71.
6. Denis Mackail, *The Story of J.M.B.* (Peter Davies, 1941), p. 57.
7. Viola Meynell (ed.), *Letters of J.M. Barrie* (Peter Davies, 1942), pp. 184–5 and 296.
8. Quoted in Islay Murray Donaldson, *The Life and Work of Samuel Rutherford Crockett* (Aberdeen University Press, 1989), p. 16.
9. Quoted in Hammerton, *Barrie: The Story of a Genius*, p. 71.
10. Lady Cynthia Asquith, *Portrait of Barrie* (James Barrie, 1954), p. 54.
11. Quoted in Hammerton, *Barrie: The Story of a Genius*, p. 74.

12. Barrie, *The Greenwood Hat* (Peter Davies, 1937), p. v.
13. Ibid., p. 134.
14. Barrie, *Margaret Ogilvy*, p. 40.
15. Doyle, *Memories and Adventures*, p. 253.
16. Barrie, *Margaret Ogilvy*, p. 49.
17. Quoted in David Carroll, *Leafing through Literature: Writers' Lives in Hertfordshire and Bedfordshire* (The Book Castle, Dunstable, 1992), p. 37.
18. Meynell (ed.), *Letters*, p. 250.
19. Ibid., p. 250.
20. Quoted in Hammerton, *Barrie: The Story of a Genius*, p. 70.
21. Meynell (ed.), *Letters*, p. 250.
22. Quoted in Hammerton, *Barrie: The Story of a Genius*, p. 294.
23. Quoted in Janet Dunbar, *J.M. Barrie: The Man Behind the Image* (Collins, 1970), p. 173.
24. Mackail, *The Story of J.M.B.*, p. 640.
25. Meynell (ed.), *Letters*, p. 301.

Eleven: Wilfred Owen and Siegfried Sassoon

1. Quoted in Jon Stallworthy, *Wilfred Owen* (Oxford University Press, 1977 edn), p. 187.
2. Harold Owen and John Bell (eds), *Wilfred Owen: Collected Letters* (Oxford University Press, 1967), pp. 471 and 473.
3. Ibid.
4. Quoted in John Stuart Roberts, *Siegfried Sassoon* (Richard Cohen Books, 1999), p. 104.

5. Siegfried Sassoon, *Sherston's Progress* (Faber & Faber, 1936), p. 11.
6. Ibid., p. 50.
7. Owen and Bell (eds), *Wilfred Owen Letters*, p. 484.
8. Siegfried Sassoon, *Siegfried's Journey* (Faber & Faber, 1945), p. 58.
9. Owen and Bell (eds), *Wilfred Owen Letters*, p. 485.
10. Ibid., p. 517.
11. Sassoon, *Sherston's Progress*, p. 12.
12. Ibid., pp. 29–30.
13. Stallworthy, *Wilfred Owen*, p. 231.
14. Sassoon, *Siegfried's Journey*, p. 59.
15. Owen and Bell (eds), *Wilfred Owen Letters*, p. 502.
16. Sassoon, *Siegfried's Journey*, p. 64.
17. Sassoon, *Sherston's Progress*, p. 147.

Twelve: An Edinburgh Review
1. Quoted in Linklater, *Edinburgh*, p. 32.
2. John Taylor, *The Pennyles Pilgrimage* (1618).
3. Quoted in Royle, *Precipitous City*, pp. 60–1.
4. Defoe, (ed. Pat Rogers), *Tour*, p. 198.
5. Ibid., p. 205.
6. Lewis Melville, *The Life and Letters of Tobias Smollett* (Faber & Gwyer, 1926), p. 218.
7. Tobias Smollett, *The Expedition of Humphry Clinker (1771)*

(Penguin English Library edn, 1967), p. 254.
8. Ibid., p. 258.
9. Ibid., p. 272.
10. Dorothy Wordsworth, *Recollections of a Tour, made in Scotland, A.D. 1803* (James Thin edn, 1981), p. 242.
11. Ibid., pp. 243–4.
12. Ibid., p. 245.
13. Edward Dowden, *The Life of Percy Bysshe Shelley* (2 vols) (Kegan Paul, Trench & Co., 1886), p. 178.
14. Ibid., p. 181.
15. Quoted in Ibid., p. 393.
16. George Borrow, *Lavengro* (1851) (Oxford University Press, 1982 edn), p. 47.
17. Ibid., pp. 53 and 47.
18. Ibid., p. 55.
19. Ibid., p. 55.
20. Daniel Green (ed.), *Cobbett's Tour in Scotland* (Aberdeen University Press, 1984), pp. 23 and 30.
21. Elizabeth Gaskell, *My Lady Ludlow and Other Tales* (1859) (John Murray edn, 1906), pp. 5 and 6.
22. Quoted in Daphne DuMaurier, *The Infernal World of Branwell Brontë* (Penguin edn, 1972), p. 53.
23. Quoted in Winifred Gerin, *Charlotte Brontë* (Oxford University Press, 1969 edn), p. 438.
24. Quoted in Rebecca Fraser, *Charlotte Brontë* (Methuen, 1988), p. 374.

25. Cockburn, *Memorials*, p. 166 and pp. 168–9.
26. Quoted in Victoria Glendinning, *Rebecca West: A Life* (Weidenfeld & Nicolson, 1987), p. 27.
27. Ibid., pp. 27–8.
28. Rebecca West, *The Judge* (1922), (Virago, 1980 edn), p. 10.
29. Ibid., p. 10.
30. Quoted in Royle, *Precipitous City*, p. 171.
31. Lady Susan Tweedsmuir (ed.), *John Buchan by His Wife and Friends* (Hodder & Stoughton, 1947), p. 36.
32. Ibid., p. 51.
33. John Buchan, *Memory Hold-the-Door* (Hodder & Stoughton, 1940), p. 244.
34. Compton Mackenzie, *My Life and Times: Octave Ten* (Chatto & Windus, 1971), pp. 12–13.
35. Linklater, *Edinburgh*, p. 129.
36. Mackenzie, *My Life and Times*, p. 97.
37. Linklater, *Edinburgh*, p. 129.
38. Quoted in Andro Linklater, *Compton Mackenzie. A Life* (Chatto & Windus, 1987), p. 320.
39. Muriel Spark, 'What Images Return', in Karl Miller (ed.), *Memoirs of a Modern Scotland* (Faber and Faber, 1970). Quoted in 'Scotland: An Anthology' (ed. Douglas Dunn), (HarperCollins, 1991), p. 118.
40. Spark, *Curriculum Vitae* (Constable, 1992), pp. 56–7.
41. Spark, *The Prime of Miss Jean Brodie* (1961), (Constable, 1993 edn), pp. 28, 11, 15, 29.
42. Norman MacCaig, *Collected Poems* (Chatto & Windus, 1985), p. 67.
43. Ibid., p. 238.
44. Joan Lingard, *The Kiss* (Allison & Busby, 2002), pp. 18–19.
45. Ibid., pp. 41, 60.

Postscript
1. Quoted in George Bruce, *Festival in the North. The Story of the Edinburgh Festival* (Robert Hale & Co., 1975), p. 18.
2. Ibid., p. 165.
3. Author's conversation with Joan Lingard, 22 October 2002.
4. *The Bookseller*, 18 December 1982.
5. Ibid., 15 January 1983.
6. Author's conversation with Jenny Brown, 23 September 2003.
7. Ibid.
8. Letter to the author from Kate Atkinson dated 18 October 2002.
9. Roy Hattersley, 'Man and Roy', in *Scotland on Sunday*, 25 August 2002.
10. Edinburgh International Book Festival email dated 26 January 2011.
11. Ibid.

BIBLIOGRAPHY

In addition to those titles mentioned in the Source Notes, the following books proved invaluable to my research. (The place of publication is London unless stated otherwise.)

Addison, William, *In the Steps of Charles Dickens*, Rich & Cowan, 1955

Aldington, Richard, *Portrait of a Rebel. The Life and Work of Robert Louis Stevenson*, Evans Bros, 1957

Bate, Walter Jackson, *Samuel Johnson*, Chatto & Windus, 1978

Bigland, Eileen, *In the Steps of George Borrow*, Rich & Cowan, 1951

Birkin, Andrew, *J.M. Barrie and the Lost Boys*, Constable & Co., 1979

Brown, Raymond Lamont, *Clarinda and the Intimate Story of Robert Burns and Agnes MacLehose*, Martin Black Publications, Dewsbury, 1968

Daiches, David, *James Boswell and His World*, Thames & Hudson, 1976

Daiches, David, *Sir Walter Scott and His World*, Thames & Hudson, 1971

Darlington, W.A., *J.M. Barrie*, Blackie & Son, 1938

De Quincey, Thomas (ed. David Wright), *Recollections of the Lakes and the Lake Poets*, Penguin English Library, 1970

Douglas, Hugh, *The Tinder Heart*, Sutton Publishing, Stroud, 1996

Drabble, Margaret (ed.), *The Oxford Companion to English Literature*, Oxford University Press, 1985

Findlay, J.R., *Personal Recollections of Thomas De Quincey*, 1886

Gerin, Winifred, *Elizabeth Gaskell*, Oxford University Press, 1976

Hibberd, Dominic, *Wilfred Owen: The Last Year 1917–1918*, Constable & Co., 1992

Kaplan, Fred, *Thomas Carlyle. A Biography*, Cambridge University Press, 1983

Kaplan, Fred, *Dickens. A Biography*, Hodder & Stoughton, 1988

Lownie, Andrew, *The Literary Companion to Edinburgh*, Methuen, 2000

Miles, Rosalind, *Ben Jonson: His Life and Work*, Routledge & Kegan Paul, 1986

Uglow, Jenny, *Elizabeth Gaskell: A Habit of Stories*, Faber & Faber, 1993

INDEX